BON COUR
MES AM

BON COURAGE, MES AMIS!

Thoughts on restoring a rural ruin

SHEILA WRIGHT

Dedicated to my dear brother David, without whom our French adventure would never have begun.

ISBN
1 901253 30 9
First published May 2002

© Sheila Wright

Published by:
Léonie Press
an imprint of
Anne Loader Publications
13 Vale Road, Hartford,
Northwich, Cheshire CW8 1PL
Gt Britain
Tel: 01606 75660   Fax: 01606 77609
e-mail: anne@leoniepress.com
Website: www.anneloaderpublications.co.uk
www.leoniepress.com

Printed by:
Anne Loader Publications

CONTENTS

ABOUT THE AUTHOR

SHEILA WRIGHT (née JONES) was born in Leicester in 1939. On leaving Wyggeston Grammar School, she trained as a primary school teacher at Bretton Hall, Yorkshire, where she met her husband Ron. They lived first in Hertfordshire, where most of their seven children were born. In 1970, the family moved into a Tudor farmhouse in the Suffolk countryside. The birth of two more children, teaching, the care of pets and various livestock, and involvement in church and village events kept them fully occupied, but Sheila found time to gain an MA in Special Educational Needs from the University of East Anglia.

The *fermette* in the Creuse was purchased in 1994 and is a fascinating retirement occupation!

Sheila's hobbies include music making, drawing and painting, reading, spending time with the family (eight grandchildren to enjoy), gardening and escapism in rural France.

ACKNOWLEDGEMENTS

The places and people in this account really exist. A few names have been changed to protect the guilty! In the main, however it is my version of The Truth!

The Wrights' Tudor home in Suffolk.
(Watercolour by the author)

THE BEGINNING

OF course, the idea was ridiculous.

A smell of damp stone and ancient dust enveloped us as our eyes became accustomed to the gloom. Here and there on the rough granite walls shadowy alcoves and battered wood frames were barely visible. Mysterious bits of string dangled from the immense beams above us, and between these beams were dark, narrow boards through which light filtered where rain had rotted them away.

One wall of the room was taken up by a vast fireplace. The recess was shallow and the hearthstone, huge and smooth, projected into the room. Nevertheless, judging by the soot-blackened flue, at least some of the smoke from past fires had managed to go up the chimney. Peering up this chimney, past various sinister blackened iron hooks, we could see a patch of bright blue sky at least thirty inches wide. So some of the water soaking the enormous flagstones on which we stood, may have come down the chimney.

Jannine, our English guide, was impatient and embarrassed at time spent showing clients this particularly desolate building. She shuffled her feet uncomfortably, remarking: "You'd think people might just clean up a bit before trying to sell a place!"

"How old do you think it is?" I asked.

"I've no idea!" Jannine shrugged her shoulders dismissively, obviously wanting to escape this dank ruin and drive us through the sunshine to some more salubrious dwelling.

Leaving the main room of the *fermette*, we had to duck around two acro-props supporting a sagging lintel onto which

Ancienne fermette, 110,000FF, as pictured in the agent's details

tons of loose granite appeared to be falling. We entered a second long cellar-like area, lit by a tiny aperture in the north wall. The earth floor was piled with hunks of granite, fallen from a crumbling wall running from front to back of the building. The jagged top of this wall was now only five feet or so high. Beyond it were a cart bay, cow shed and stable, all under the one long roof.

Looking around us we could see rectangular holes in the walls, where joists supporting long-gone upper floors had rested. Now the "room" was open to the rafters thirty feet or more above us. But my eye was held by a beautifully fashioned recess in the thick granite wall, surrounded by smooth dressed stone. What kind of life had long-ago people lived in this building?

With evident relief, Jannine led us through a low door encased by massive stone frame and lintel, into the fresh air. The high wall to the right of this doorway showed an alarming

2

jagged crack running twenty feet from top to bottom.

"Is that crack dangerous?" I asked.

"I've seen much worse – if it's settled it's probably OK. A builder would tell you."

On the rough land in front of this long-abandoned *fermette*, neighbours had allowed an array of spectacular junk to accumulate. Rabbit hutches leaned on old cars, rotten timber and sheets of plastic. Loose piles of stone made our way precarious. Somewhere under all this were the remains of building materials: sand and gravel on a black plastic sheet. Some intrepid soul had attempted restoration, but had admitted defeat. I could imagine his wife's disapproval: "If you're going to spend every weekend messing about on that smelly old ruin, I'm leaving you!"

Outside, I could once again feast my eyes on the exterior stone stairway which had first awakened my interest when looking at photos in the agents' office.

"We can't go up there – the floor's rotten," said Jannine hurriedly, noticing my interest in the rough doorway above, leading to the "bedroom".

With relief, she led us to her car, obviously feeling that anyone who wanted to spend more than five minutes in this derelict place was stark staring mad.

And this was how the story began.

THE SEARCH

"COME on – we have to meet the agent at ten o'clock, don't forget..."

"We're sure to get lost at least once – who's got the map?"

We wrapped a breakfast *croissant* or two in a paper napkin, with a few sealed packs of butter, marmalade and jam; Formule 1 Hotel breakfasts are generous but we were late again. Off for a *rendez-vous* with an English ex-patriate earning a few extra francs by showing foolish English dreamers like me around ramshackle country properties in various states of decay.

Today's guide, Charles, invited us into a shabby car decorated with sweet wrappers, dog hairs, and bundles of agents' papers. Charles wore a lived-in donkey jacket, and hummed vaguely to himself as he drove us along obscure lanes and muddy woodland tracks. He would not worry whether we got as far as buying a property or not; he was paid expenses and a little more for his time, and obviously had been on many a wild goose chase.

"It's round this corner, I think..." Charles nonchalantly indicated another crumbly cottage, one front wall sagging into its own cellar. We peered into a musty abyss under the stairs.

"It's quite cheap, only 60,000 francs".

"It must have been lovely once – but all these outbuildings don't go with it, surely?"

"Some do, some don't – and there's a right of way to that old piggery, across the garden here."

"Oh well, let's get on to the next one, shall we?"

We saw a bewildering array of cottages, barns and farmhouses. The most solidly constructed were the farm buildings. Human habitations obviously were of secondary importance. You had to be a visionary to appreciate what they might become; the cheap end of the market is no place for the faint-hearted.

Many appealed to me, but none was just right. An old forge, in a tiny village high up in the woods near Bourganeuf, contained a mass of blacksmith's artefacts. Huge bellows, immense cauldrons, a workshop crammed with heavy tools, all could be ours. And in the back garden on the hillside stood the bullock-shoeing shed. The bleached wood frame into which the hapless bullocks were driven and strapped tight, stood rock firm, a nostalgic reminder of a way of life gone for ever.

Other sheds, cellars and kitchens contained metal-bound kegs and barrels, a grindstone, old farm carts and wagons, scythes, cast-iron pots, earthenware bowls and jars for cream

Outhouse treasure

and cheesemaking. Our various guides regarded these (together with various soggy mattresses which adorned the bedrooms) as so much junk. None of these "bits and pieces" were mentioned in the printed details. An English collector or dealer would have had a field day.

We were fascinated. But always, there were snags. Several of the houses were split-level: two storeys at the front, but only one at the back since the walls straddled a steep hillside. And where did the water run, what happened to the foundations (if they existed at all) in these conditions? In one case, hillside streams appeared to run through and under the house, emerging in a series of runnels into water troughs hewn out of solid rock, for the use of both humans and their livestock.

Other cottages had very little land, allowing no possibility of septic tank installation. Sometimes, one wall of the house formed the boundary with an adjoining plot – could we be sure of access for building maintenance? Too many were in delightful spots but opened directly onto tarmac roads. One pleasant semi-renovated property was shaded by a neighbour's high stone wall on one side, dead-looking coniferous woods on two more sides, and a jungle of Japanese Knotweed in its "garden".

One terraced cottage boasted a fine fireplace, but above this lurked a retractable metal ladder leading up to the "conveniences". When pulled down, this eyesore of a ladder led from the hearth to a murky attic where a wash-basin stood crookedly under the eaves. An Elsan graced the lean-to barn alongside. This cottage had its own earthy *cave* under the garden. The old man next door became quite excited at the prospect of neighbours, but I had my doubts.

Undoubtedly, the best bargain in terms of quantity of land and buildings for the money, was at Rimondeix. This substantial barn of mellow granite faced south, a picturesque vine clinging to the rough sun-soaked stone. But included in the sale was a two-acre plot of boggy land, waist-high in nettles, on which stood a further low *fermette* consisting of farmhouse and adjoining barns. This was crammed full of old furniture, timber, stones and *bric-à-brac*, and the roof was ominously wavy. I would not have had the nerve to go home to an unsuspecting husband with the news that I (or we) were now responsible for so much muddle and confusion, even for only 85,000 francs!

There was one day left. My companions, daughter Elisabeth and daughter-in-law Jane, kept me in good spirits and seemed to try hard not to make discouraging comments. I had one last house to visit, near Charron in the Auzance district. The picture this time was in colour, showing blue skies above a charming simple building of golden stone. The description was brief: "Stone barn with tiled roof, and adjoining land (2040 sq.m.) Water is connected; there is an electricity pole nearby. A small stream runs less than 50m away, and joins a larger stream approximately 200m away."

Maybe this would be the one? We went to sleep full of expectation.

3

DECISION

"WATCH out – the road's all bends and I think last night was cold enough for a frost."

"Yes, but it must be OK by now, nearly ten o'clock and the sun blazing down."

We were speeding through thickly wooded countryside, the maples and beech already turning to glorious autumn hues. The route led eastwards through twisting valleys, around hillsides hiding each new vista from view, causing sudden exclamations of delight:

"Look... there, on that hill... there's a tower sticking up... yes, it's a *château*! What a view!"

"Yes, in good condition, too, by the looks of it. Most of them look a bit battered but I bet someone still lives in that one. Move your head while I take a photo!"

Rounding a corner on the outskirts of a village, we were stopped by three aggressive looking folk waving sticks. Obediently, we stopped. Was this a hold-up? What had we done wrong? There was an old man, and his wife, and an alarmingly pregnant young woman (she wore a tight jumper and trousers). But they weren't really interested in us. They just wanted their cows to cross the road safely. Four cows lumbered in front of us, nudging each other, each a different colour and painfully heavy with milk. We waited for the rest of the herd... but no, we were waved on with a smile. Three people to fetch in four cows! We drove on.

"Read those instructions again, Liz, will you?"

"D4 through Mainsat – in Auzances, go past Credit Agricole Bank (left), 50 yards after turn left ('Centre Equestre') – 200

A house I didn't buy (taken from agent's details)

yards on right hand side, house back from the road with out-door steps in front. Park in drive. Go up steps, ring bell and go in, ask for Madame Gauthier".

Madame Gauthier was young, petite and very chic. She drove a rather smart car and we followed, away down lanes, over bridges, right off the beaten track. We would never have found this place on our own. At last, with a bank of beeches on our left and a steep wooded hillside on our right, we stopped. Madame didn't really want to get out of her car – she wore high heels and the ground was sodden. We could hear a rushing river to our left. There stood the barn, on our right, leaning against the soggy hillside. Yes, it was a beautiful spot, no other dwelling in sight, and the barn was really attractive – at last!

But as we approached, my heart sank and my hopes faded. We squelched along (the "small stream" seemed to have spread!) spotting more and greater defects as we neared the cracking walls. The brickwork surrounding doors and win-

9

dows was crumbling. Some bricks had lost the battle against gravity. Tiles were loose. Inside, water dripped continuously. The huge wooden doors facing the hillside at the back were loose and sagging.

When I remarked that the barn appeared to be leaning on the damp hillside, Madame suggested that a fire might help to dry the building out... I was not convinced. She stayed in her car while we took a short walk further up the valley, where a towering stone mill stood, sound but vast, its wheel damaged and obviously abandoned.

This was the last house on our list. One more day to go before we set off for the north coast and the Ferry. I had hoped this barn would be just right; disconsolate, I tried hard to persuade myself, against all reason, that we could somehow make it safe and sound. After all, it was the most romantic setting we had seen as well as the last property on our list.

But even I possess a little common sense! So we said *merci* and *au revoir* to Madame, who was obviously relieved to have done her duty by these unfashionable, clumsy Brits who apparently liked walking through mud, and drove west.

I decided to spend the last day having a second look at a few properties, without any guide to cramp my style. We were limited to those we could find, and I felt vaguely half-hearted about all these. There was no pull of desire, no yearning to make any house my own.

I knew which one I had liked best, however. But what had I said to my husband before leaving home? "Don't worry, if I buy one, it will be a small house that doesn't need much work!" And the one I really wanted to revisit was the *fermette* at Pradelette. It was big, and any novice could see there was no end to the work needed. Anyway, I had no idea how to find it... I remembered only that it was in the commune of Clugnat, an area ten miles in circumference.

Obstinate as ever, we set out in roughly the right direction. The late October evening was drawing in. We rounded a corner, and suddenly I saw the roof, half way up a hillside, just visible behind another farmhouse. Yes, that was it, the left side (*grange*) slate, and the right side (*maison*) red pantiles. Finding it so easily felt like a good omen.

We hastily parked the car, and scurried along a farm track to gaze again at those outside steps and the antique small-paned front window. Pushing open the door we saw once again corners of flagstones beneath the rubble, and on walls and fireplace, those mysterious alcoves and cubby holes. Climbing the steps, we peered into the "bedroom" for the first time; it was huge with marvellous roof timbers (but damp underfoot, holes in the floor and crumbly open "windows" that had never seen glass). We entered the cart shed, with its huge feeding-troughs along one wall. From here we could look through small interior stable windows, to where intriguing shadowy shapes filled the padlocked stable – surely an old horse-collar hung there? Heaped-up, heavy dark furniture filled every corner, some shrouded in cobwebby material. We climbed a battered wood ladder to the dim hay-loft above, and were amazed to find it had a lovely tiled floor.

Well, I thought, I must not be too stupid. I must at least discover whether water and electricity are available. From the farm buildings behind came the tinkle of bells. Following the sound, we found a milking shed. Twenty or so contented Friesians chewed the cud, each with a brass bell hanging from a leather strap around its neck. A pleasant-faced woman in a blue overall was busy feeding calves from a bucket. She smiled, she understood my French – but she directed us to another farmhouse, where "Andrée" was sure to know. Andrée emerged, all smiles, wiping her hands on her flowered overall, and told us yes, there had certainly been electric light; and a water supply for the horses emerged at floor level in the stable (door locked). We hurried back, reassured and excited. The view across the valley from the top of the stairs was amazing, despite the bulk of the newer granite farmhouse further down the slope which partly obstructed "our" view. And on the washing line of this farmhouse hung small children's garments

– jeans, a red sweater, a little dress. Somehow, this seemed another friendly sign.

As we studied previous properties, we had occasionally found ourselves silently watched by villagers, sometimes in a slightly furtive or suspicious manner. In this village we felt a warmth of welcome mixed with the natural curiosity. People smiled at us, people had time for us.

I was hooked!

4

"TO BUY OR NOT TO BUY?"

DRIVING north to the coast, my mind was in a whirl. I knew what I wanted to do, and I also knew it was a foolish and unreasonable desire. I wanted to buy the *fermette* at Pradelette.

It would be an impulse buy based on a total lack of knowledge of what restoration would entail. I am a natural optimist but even I could not help realising it would be a long struggle with many setbacks. Also how would I explain my choice to my husband? I knew that he secretly hoped my urge to buy a rural retreat in France would evaporate when faced with the hazards of actual properties, instead of the tantalising eulogies of estate agents. I had certainly learned that all estate agents' photographs were taken from the best possible angle on the sunniest of days, also that these agents were apparently totally blind to the most glaring of structural deficiencies.

The reasons NOT to buy were legion. We already own, and live in, a beautiful Tudor farmhouse with a garden that likes to take a leap for the wild whenever we turn our backs. We are fully involved in the village and surrounded by friends. We have seven children and a growing number of grandchildren to occupy our time. I had a demanding teaching post which might have been too much for me if it were not that my husband had taken early retirement and enjoys being a "house-husband". Why make our lives even more complicated?

The reasons to buy were few, but pressing. The idea had taken root since my dear brother, many years earlier, had asked me if we would like to go shares with him and his wife in the purchase of a French property. Reluctantly, we had to say no, having at that time absolutely no "spare" cash. But we had greatly enjoyed our visits to his rustic retreat near Bordeaux, with its vine-covered walls and sunny position high over the sunflowers. Our first visits had been relaxed and carefree, with a bucket "shower" in a tree in the garden, lizards and beetles sharing the "indoors" which seemed almost to merge into the "outdoors", and the cries of owls and wild things of the night entering the small glass-less windows.

Now, several years on, their farmhouse had become increasingly civilised and safe. The romantic *pigeonnier* and the old stable were still untouched, and the welcome was as warm as ever. But the house had become rather smart and this was not the atmosphere I wanted.

So, I started receiving the "French Property News" publication. Being by nature a dreamer, I was increasingly obsessed by the delightful pictures and descriptions of "bargain buys" in remote French countryside. I dreamed about isolated farmhouses that spoke of the past; cottages surrounded by grass and trees; locations in which I might wander the morning garden in my nightie if the mood took me.

Thanks to a gift from my mother, at last I had a small amount of cash put by. I was also getting rapidly older, having passed my fiftieth birthday (although I never quite believed it!). So I felt it was a case of now or never.

One house-hunting visit seemed hardly adequate – there must be other non-touristy, inexpensive country areas, with hundreds of more suitable properties just waiting to be discovered. But this one trip to France, with ferry, petrol and hotels, had burned up five hundred pounds of my carefully saved cash. If I carried on looking, my money would evaporate and I would be even older, with even less time ahead to enjoy whatever property was "just right"!

So by the time we were home my mind was made up. I telephoned Guy, a teacher who provided not only details of properties but also invaluable help with purchase and legal matters in both French and English. I told him I wanted to make an offer of 100,000FF on condition that Monsieur Auclair, the vendor, would have the roof and leaking chimney-stack repaired.

The repairs were made but the price remained at 110,000FF. This I accepted, and several long months of waiting elapsed. Six months later the legal business was complete and a proxy (employee of the local *notaire*) was appointed to sign the *"Compromis de Vente"* in my absence.

I didn't know which emotion was uppermost – excitement, panic, or just sheer terror! Whatever deep water was I entering?

One Saturday morning as "the day" approached I lay in bed late, savouring the knowledge that I did not have to leap up, try to look respectable and efficient, and make my way to the village where a class of infants awaited me. The phone rang. It was Guy.

"I've just had the *notaire*, M. Cerclier, on the phone. He tells me someone else has made a higher offer for the *fermette* at Pradelette, and if you don't increase your offer you may lose it. What do you want me to say?"

What did I want to say? There was a note of irony in Guy's voice; probably he, like me, suspected the "other buyer" was a myth. But I could not be sure. I felt I was already being reckless enough. I had cashed in a Life Assurance Policy (to the apparent consternation of the finance company who kept writing to express their surprise and ask if I was SURE I wanted to miss out on the fantastic returns I would receive if I waited until I was dead!). I was already committed to spending more than my original intention. So reluctantly, I gave Guy my answer:

"No, I can't offer more, I'm over-stretched as it is. I have to stick at 110,000."

I put the phone down and lay back on the pillows. A feeling of deep sadness enveloped me as I thought how near I had come to owning a corner of rural France. Now it was just a dream lost; probably I would never try again. Mixed with this sadness was an unmistakeable, traitorous flood of relief – what difficulties, what problems, what decisions had I avoided by

NOT buying the *fermette*? I shut my eyes...

The phone rang again. What now? It was Guy speaking:

"M. Cerclier just rang. The other buyer has withdrawn. So they're signing the agreement today – in an hour or so the *fermette* will be yours!"

5

NOTRE PREMIER SÉJOUR

"LOOK – there are cows in the garden!"

"Surely not – oh yes, a lovely brown one, and a white one with spots. That's strange!"

"You must have made a mistake, you only bought half the building, the farm end belongs to someone else!"

"No, I'm sure it's all mine, it's on all the plans. It was definitely the whole building with grass all around on three sides!"

"Look, there's a piece of binder twine fixed to the wall by the big barn door and going over to that plum tree – that must be the boundary!"

Our anxious discussion was brought to an end by the arrival of a flustered overall-clad lady who appeared from the farmhouse south of ours. She hastily untied the binder twine and shooed her two cows into a neighbouring field, coming back to apologise with many a *"Pardonnez-moi, s'il vous plaît!"* for the presence of her cows on our land.

With great relief, we assured her it didn't matter, and introduced ourselves. This was Nicole, who turned out to be the most considerate and *gentille* of neighbours as the years rolled by.

We were a party of three: myself, my husband Ron, and my sister's son Tim. We had driven down in our ancient van, equipped with camping gear, sundry tools and a box of food, for our first summer sojourn at Pradelette.

Ever since April, when the signed *Compromis de Vente* arrived at our Suffolk home, I had been consumed by a mixture of emotions. Exhilaration vied with nervous anxiety – what had I done? How could I justify this reckless, rather random purchase, to my pragmatic husband (a typical "Capricorn" and a Yorkshireman to boot). I had only seen the *fermette* briefly, twice, and had not even entered some areas. Would the whole thing now be revealed to me as a terrible mistake? Would it be idyll, or nightmare?

Fortunately, the trip down had been pleasant. When only eight miles from our destination, we had stopped the van in amazement to admire the stunning *château* at Boussac. This powerful fortified building towers over a terrifying cliff. How many menials had met a sudden death during its construction, we wondered? The bravado of building so tall a structure in such a position was breathtaking. Somehow this awesome sight seemed to convey a certainty that we had come to a very special place. We drove on.

Thank goodness! Yes, the *fermette* still held strong immediate appeal for me! And the neighbours had kindly cleared the old cars and so on from among the tall grass and weeds. Even my husband had to agree that the western end, at least, looked almost as solid as the *château*. But he did not hide his doubts about the "house" end. Quite apart from the heaps of rubble which covered the floors, there was the obvious odour of damp everywhere: rising from the stone flags of the main room, the earth floor of the smaller room – which smelled like a dank cellar – and above, rotten floorboards and holes in the "bedroom" floor. We quickly decided that the best place to set up our "camp" was the business end – the former stable, cowshed and tractor bay.

Tim climbed the rickety wooden ladder to the *grenier*, carrying his sleeping bag. We lugged our blow-up mattress and bedding into the stable. I had brought candlesticks and a good supply of candles and matches, and we set these up around our sleeping quarters.

Ron's eyes were constantly drawn to the many glaring defects – the stable door with its missing bottom planks; the disintegrating garden wall leaning on the damp northern side of the building, from which sprang nettles, ivy, brambles and

South-east corner of our fermette

elderberry in exuberant profusion. I had to admit it was unfortunate that even the inside north wall of the stable was adorned with rampant greenery! Trying to justify my folly, I took the line that we need not worry unduly about the state of the building – it would not actually fall down, and we could simply enjoy it as a base for camping while exploring the French countryside. But as the days went by, Ron's practical nature took over and various repairs were made. He mended the doors (ample planking lay around) and made painstaking repairs to the rotten upper floor of the house. The local builders' yard could not supply tongue-and-groove boarding as narrow as the original, so his patching up was a work of extreme inventiveness.

We got to know the neighbours, who were endlessly generous with gifts of vegetables, eggs and advice. We visited local beauty spots and historic ruins. We cooked on a camp stove; tasty meals with wine to give the continental atmosphere. We made a temporary chemical toilet from a large bucket, a toilet seat and fluid which smelled deliciously of blackcurrants! Ron was adept at digging deep holes in corners of the "garden" for this – he had already used his strimmer to create paths through the wilderness where needed. After a few days, our eldest son David joined us, and we explored local bathing spots, mainly areas of the River Creuse, in which we swam with the fish, and discreetly washed ourselves with soap and flannel in the shallows!

One night, we experienced the first of many electric storms. The village is on the northern slopes of a long wooded valley, and humidity eventually gives way to violent storms which thunder up and down the length of the valley. Sometimes these storms are heralded with "a rushing, mighty wind" of biblical proportions – the roaring of the wind is enough to wake sleepers even before the continuous thunder, sheet lightning and torrential rain begin. We awoke to hear rushing water, not only outside, but inside too. It flowed in a torrent just past our pillow, along the groove running from north to south in the centre of the stable floor, and out under the door!

We made many discoveries, some of them delightful, as when, removing the tangle of ivy on the stable wall, we discovered a tiny prehistoric-looking window in the three foot thick wall. It was divided in half by a long smooth piece of granite, wedged top-to-bottom and looking like a mystic standing stone. And to the left of the enormous fireplace a metal guard lifted off to reveal a bread oven, fully two metres in diameter, with a domed ceiling created by narrow bricks or tiles fixed sideways on. We later discovered that hundreds of butterflies hibernated in this oven; and among the assorted junk we found a long wooden peel for placing the loaves, and hung this in its rightful place above the fireplace.

Curiously, there was only one marked boundary to our land. One narrow end of the building abuts the farm track, the other, a field with a wire fence. On the two long sides, weeds and various gnarled, lichen-covered fruit trees grew. Some of these trees were long dead and made a good bonfire. Others hung with fruit. But where were our long boundaries?

Neighbours on the north and south long sides were glad to help. With many a gallic gesture indicating "left-hand down a bit!" they showed us the official line; on the north, stretching from a plum tree to a distant pylon (but stopping at the wire fence enclosing a cow pasture), and on the other, between a bullace tree and a small disc set in the sandy farm track. Both lines were marked out carefully with binder twine and stakes. I was delighted to find our "garden" was larger than expected. There was at least thirty feet in front of our property – wide enough to allow the planting of trees and shrubs to soften the view of plain granite wall, and provide some privacy.

After ten days, we shut up the *fermette*, said reluctant farewells to our new friends, the neighbours, and drove down to Bordepaille, near Monségur, to celebrate the thirtieth wedding anniversary of my brother and his wife. There we revelled – two spit-roast lambs and a great deal of red wine, summer nights amid the noise of the crickets and the chatter of both French and English voices.

And so ended our first *séjour* as novice owners of a French *fermette*.

6

EXPLORATIONS
AND EXPERIENCES

MY knowledge of France, this wonderful enticing country, was and still is quite limited. After all, there are many beautiful corners of the British Isles of which I know nothing. And now I had acquired a second home in a fairly random manner, in this huge country that was largely a mystery to me.

My first foray into France had taken place forty years earlier. In the 1950s I went with my sister Margo on a fortnight's "exchange", living with my pen-friend Odile and her parents in the countryside bordering Rouen. This was an eye-opener to us, startlingly different from our customary life in a comfortable leafy suburb of a Midlands town.

Odile and her parents lived in a tiny house set in the middle of a two-acre garden. This house had been laboriously constructed brick by brick, room by room, by this brave and determined couple, who had neither an abundance of money nor of time. They had started with the good square kitchen, always the hub of a French family home. Later they added, at the side, a tiny entrance hall with just room for the stairs which would be built later. A minute "best room" or *salon* adjoined this hall – there was just space for an upright piano which I think was for them a proud symbol of culture and gentility. Later, a first floor was added – tiny landing plus parental bedroom. As Odile grew older a second floor grew above this – another tiny landing leading to her own bedroom, which we were to share, directly under the bare roof tiles. The ground floor was twice the area of the floors above, so the house appeared as a kind of brick tower rising out of rampant greenery.

In true French style, they had created an orchard around their cherished home: not only the apples, pears and plums that we were used to, but also cherries and peaches (maybe apricots as well, time has blurred some detail). There was of course a magnificent vegetable plot and every conceivable type of soft fruit alongside. In the centre of the garden rose an enormous mountain of vegetable (and other!) waste.

Odile's garments were clean but extremely well-worn and much mended. There were no labour-saving gadgets of any kind. The parents had a market stall where they sold boots, slippers and shoes. They would leave home around 5am, arrive in the market square of Rouen or some other neighbouring town, and set to work unloading the van, setting up the wooden stall, and displaying their wares – shoes and boots removed from their boxes and carefully arranged to tempt passers-by. By 7.30am the market would be in full swing. We accompanied them only a couple of times and found it distinctly boring, as it was not thought proper for young girls to wander among the crowd, even in a threesome.

It seemed to us that very few pairs of shoes were ever sold. And at 2pm it was time to start all the tedious packing up and stacking away of goods and stall – a wearisome task day after day.

Once back home, the important business of life commenced – this was of course, the preparation and enjoyment of the evening meal. I say "evening" because although Madame was busy by four o'clock, the meal would still be in progress at 11pm! It was all very traditional, but amazing to us.

We would each sit down around the kitchen table to some kind of starter – perhaps melon or *pâté*. Then, plates wiped with bread, Madame might ask if we would like lettuce? If the answer was yes (and we were too polite ever to say no) she would get up, go into the garden, come back bearing a large muddy lettuce, and proceed to wash it carefully and toss the crisp leaves in some delicious home-made dressing. Then we would be given a helping – on the plate already used. Melon followed by lettuce is not too difficult; but to us uninitiated English misses, courses such as snails (yes, we really ate them!) or shell-fish, followed later by rich pastry or peaches and cream eaten from the same plate was really peculiar, and quite difficult to organise if you happened not to have been able to swallow every mouthful of snail, even pushed down by bread!

One day, we were asked around five o'clock whether we would prefer chicken or rabbit. I forget which we asked for – but Madame bustled out, muffled squawks or squeals were heard, and to our horror she reappeared carrying a warm bundle of fur or feathers, and got busy with her knife at the sink! We were used to rabbits in garden hutches – but only as mollycoddled pets. However we were hungry and the eventual smells were good, and we truly appreciated her efforts.

I remember my first oysters, and mussels cooked in red wine, also what to us was a gruesome mixture – raw egg mixed well with cold macaroni! One day, we had artichoke hearts, the leaves pulled off and dipped in rich sauce. I was trying hard to be a good guest but this was not a flavour I liked. Feeling queasy and needing some fresh air, I went over to the open window and breathed deeply, only to feel even more nauseous! Looking out, I saw that all waste from our meal had been thrown out of this window into the chicken run which adjoined the house at this point! At least the chickens were happy.

Unfortunately, my stomach found all these new tastes and textures coming so thick and fast, a bit too much. Seeing that I was really under par, our hosts called in the neighbours from the house opposite. These were a group of ungainly unmarried sisters – apparently the family had numbered eleven, and many had stayed at home into adulthood. Their house was minute, like a small pre-fab, and stood on a tiny plot. I could not understand how so many large people could fit into so small a house. Anyway, these kindly neighbours tenderly laid hands on my stomach – right on my naked skin! This was quite an embarrassment to a self-conscious teenager. But I was ordered to lie on the bed while "healing hands" stroked and massaged my rumbling tummy! The sisters were in fact kindness itself but to me it was all very odd.

Margaret and I quickly learned to eat plenty of bread for breakfast, as sometimes nothing was offered after this until the evening feast commenced. The morning hot chocolate was served in wide bowls and, instead of drinking as from a cup, we learned to dip our buttered bread into it and suck. To me this made rather a mushy and greasy meal but I did need to eat! Margo and I soon learned to wander the garden in search of fallen fruit to bridge the long gap between meals.

This house had no bathroom of any kind. On each landing, outside the two bedrooms, stood two white enamel buckets, one for washing, the other for all "natural functions!" The water was stone cold and was brought up from the kitchen. We were given soap with which to wash our undies in these buckets. Full buckets were emptied, not down a deep dark hole under cover of darkness, but onto the high waste heap in the garden. We were embarrassed that dear monsieur should have to do this on our behalf, but to him it was quite normal. What I could not understand was how the huge family over the road managed on their tiny plot!

Odile's father had a primitive battered car as well as the van. In this car, he drove us to see the Normandy beaches, Dunkirk, and the tapestry at Bayeux. We also visited a distant relative who lay pale and wan in a huge double bed in a downstairs room, having given birth to a scrap of a baby. From the expressions and tone of voice of these exhausted and struggling cousins, we gained the impression that the baby's arrival was regarded as a burden as well as a joy. Life was very very hard. The place and its people had been sadly ravaged by the War.

Monsieur had various pleasures – one was his ownership of various odd small plots of land. Several were some distance from his home, others among local houses. We would be driven for miles, only to stop by a small fenced-in area of rough land. Beaming all over his face and making expansive gestures, he led us to understand that each tiny patch was his. After the devastating devaluation of the franc, land was regarded as the only safe investment. After all, what use were banks if your thousands of francs were suddenly peanuts? His other pleasure seemed to be studying the newspaper for details of deaths and injuries in rail or road crashes, and gleefully announcing to all present just how many people had come to grief that day!

Odile stayed with us in England, and must have been as bewildered by our lifestyle as we were by hers. We kept up the correspondence, intermittently, over the years. In the 1980s we visited her with all seven of our children (plus an eighth, friend of daughter Anne). We received a wonderful welcome. The family fortunes had risen unbelievably. A pair of sedate semi-detached houses stood in a leafy residential district of Rouen. Approached through neat gardens, each house boasted garage, boiler room and workshop in the basement, and wide steps wound upwards to a gracious front door. In one house lived Odile with chemist husband Michel, and two children. In the other lived Odile's aged parents – by this date dim of vision, bent and gnarled, but with true contentment etched into their lived-in faces. These diminutive survivors from a vanished world still clung to their traditional priorities of life. Proudly they showed us several miniscule rows of vegetables, lovingly tended in the (now suburban-style) flower garden. They seemed delighted by our arrival and searched out faded black-and-white photographs taken during that first visit so long ago.

Most extraordinary of all was the fact that the address had not changed. The town of Rouen had grown and grown, spreading its tentacles into what was once a rural area. These two smart houses were built on the original two-acre plot! The parents' determination and dogged industry had paid off. Never did two people more deserve good fortune.

Over the years, there have been other visits both ways – Odile and husband Michel would be in England attending conferences, often at Cambridge university, and touring in their caravan; and they would call on us.

In her early fifties, Odile suffered a severe stroke. She had to go into a nursing home for rehabilitation, where with expert treatment she regained both speech and movement to a large extent. The shock of this brought on depression and a terrible lack of confidence, but Michel is a gentle, patient and loving husband who has gradually encouraged her to live life again. As I write this I am not proud of myself since I have selfishly neglected this dear friend.

The last time we visited was in the early nineties. We were royally entertained, but since her illness, being hostess requires immense concentration and effort. We accompanied Odile on a shopping trip which seemed to involve the most minute inspection of every grape or cheese or mussel to be bought, so that it was late afternoon when we arrived home. Odile disappeared into the kitchen, declining help from anyone, while we tried not to watch the clock (our ferry left Dieppe at 1am). A splendid meal began around 9.30pm and we did want to do it justice! We ate oysters, mussels cooked in red wine, salmon, lamb, various vegetables, some odorous cheeses, *gâteau* and fruit. All these are favourites of mine (but preferably spread over a week!) but Ron doesn't enjoy any shell-fish. At last we were able to leave, trying not to show undue haste and to say all the things that friendship and courtesy demand.

We drove like maniacs to the port and just swerved up the ramp in time. The best seats were all taken and we sat unpleasantly near the engines with a strong waft of diesel fumes to add to the discomfort of rough seas and replete stomachs!

The longer we have owned the *fermette,* the more obsessed we have become with finishing work there. We occasionally find ourselves in or near Rouen but it is not our favourite town for route-finding. There seem to be dozens of ways to get through or round the town and we never find the same one twice. On one journey, we will be swallowed up by a sudden gaping tunnel, to emerge blinking with the worst traffic behind us, rejoicing at our cleverness. Then the next time, we will be directed in circles, or rather in squares, across the Seine, through traffic lights and one way roads, only to find another sign sending us back over the river half a mile from where we started. It is weird – we can't help suspecting there are evil town councillors watching and trying to hide their gleeful amusement at our antics. Rouen is also one of the districts where we inadvertently find ourselves on an autoroute, without money, and fast approaching a toll. So we just don't want to hang around at this stage of our journey if we can help it. But we have told Odile and Michel (now like us, grandparents) all about our Creuse venture and maybe one day they will visit us.

To return to my saga of early French experiences; my next visit was by yacht. At seventeen, I was an enthusiastic Sea Ranger (branch of the Girl Guides) despite living so far from the sea. I joined a trip on a converted Brixham fishing trawler. There was an engine, but it was only used in dire emergencies. We had a crew: a mate-cum-cook, and a Captain. He would direct us as to what rope we should haul on to adjust the heavy rust-coloured sails. We didn't really know what we were doing, we just blindly obeyed orders. I had a mnemonic to help me recall which was "Starboard": Starboard Right, S-R, as in "Sea Ranger". Previously, our Ranger excursions had been confined to canoes on the local canal.

Our trip was delayed due to bad weather. We were stranded in Weymouth. We seemed to keep meeting boys. One of these was really more a man, an American seaman, who took a great fancy to me and couldn't get over my "cute accent". He was a bit uninhibited and I was getting nervous; but we finally loosed anchor, bound for Alderney. What a delectable island! I was in seventh heaven. The rocky coasts were a little marred by hunks of wartime concrete and defensive barbed wire, but I could not take my eyes off the little colour-washed cottages and the green landscape. I have an abiding inner snapshot of a padre in flowing black cape and black biretta, feeding a vast flock of pigeons in a quaint car-less street. (I have never been back. Would I now see camp-sites and caravans?)

Well, on we went, headed for Cherbourg. The sea was rough; some Sea Rangers had given up being intrepid and lay groaning in their bunks, pleading for an early release through death. I stayed on deck, enjoying the fresh salt winds, and discovering I could be quite neatly sick over the side and immediately feel better for a short while! We were glad to dock. Cherbourg was

"Terministe", adieu! August 1956

enchanting. We spent evenings in small café-bars full of French sailors, where the throbbing romantic music of soft drums and plaintive violins was heard. I loved it. But once again we got entangled with men! French sailors this time, stylish in their navy outfits, light-blue stripes on the chest and red tassel on their sailor hats. I can't remember the name of the lad who attached himself to me; but I do remember he took me to a rifle-shooting range and won trinkets which he presented to me. When the time came for us to leave, he pulled the red tassel from his hat and gave it to me, swearing undying love. Back at home I received some alarmingly passionate letters from him, and I still possess a tiny silver-and-blue crucifix on a silver chain that he sent me for Christmas.

Our glimpse of Cherbourg and port life was tantalisingly brief. Going home, we all had to take a turn at the wheel. I remember the cold Dog Watch, and being instructed as to the exact point on the compass where the twinkling lights of Portland Bill should be.

It was to be twenty years before I returned to France.

7

HOLIDAYS HOME AND AWAY

I WAS married at twenty and life carried us onward willy-nilly. Ron had worked seven years on farms, but had since trained as a teacher of music. Thus it came about that our first two homes were farm cottages, where in lieu of rent, Ron milked a herd of cows two weekends out of three. I had always yearned to live in the "real" country so was well content. But when the farmer went bankrupt and we became homeless, there was nothing for it but to scrape together some funds and buy our own home. This was a minute bungalow, four rooms each nine by eleven foot six, plus a tatty lean-to kitchen tacked on the back. It had a lovely long garden backing on to common land, so I was happy to put up with damp and mouldy walls and ceilings (clay soil, no cavity walls) and the distinct absence of heat in the winter. Ron created a stairway within an unused chimney space, and converted the loft, which became the largest room in the house, but with limited standing space! We were all right; but I never could view this as a long-term home.

We had no car, no television, no washing machine, no fridge even – this was not so unusual in the 1960s. But "proper" holidays were out, even days out were difficult with a clutch of small children. Several times we "minded" a small family farm for friends – just a few acres in a beautiful setting, a house cow, ducks on a pond, pigeons, rabbits and a vegetable garden to care for. I loved this, we feasted on blackberries and cream; but with a constant stream of nappies and small clothes to wash, toddlers underfoot and no transport, this was a fairly hard-working holiday! Of course we were able to stay with relatives and my parents were ever-welcoming and would come and fetch us in their Dormobile.

By the time our fourth child was a toddler, we had acquired a small Morris Minor, and so attempted camping. This too was a struggle, and I recall coming home a few days early from Devon, where we had installed ourselves in a soggy field near Slapton Sands. We simply could not dry the nappies – Devon was shrouded in a clinging mist and we resorted to driving along with damp nappies draped over the seat-backs and the heater on, just to get one or two dry enough to use!

Time went by; we had one "holiday" in a Folkestone bed-and-breakfast, but since Ron was at the time supervising twenty teenage boys from Watford, this was not really a taste of freedom! He also took boys on canoe camping trips along the Thames and the Wye but there was no way I could go along. He went to Paris with a group of children another year, during the time of the Algerian troubles. A terrorist shot several men dead right outside the hotel, rather putting Ron off the responsibility of these trips! Besides, I wanted him to spend holiday times with me and the children. We lived between Watford and St. Albans, and I was depressed to see the M1 come into our village. Also the oak woods were being transformed into housing estates – "little boxes", as the song goes. I wanted to move.

My mother's cousin Barbara lived in Suffolk, in a heavily beamed Tudor farmhouse with enough acres to support a small dairy herd. We were often invited there, and sometimes had the use of two old caravans to augment our smallish tent. Ron would help Bernard around the farm, and sometimes Barbara would find time to take the rest of us to the coast (I had not yet learned to drive). Suffolk was a revelation to me: not flat, but gently rolling countryside dotted with colour-washed villages, many thatched cottages, and a slower pace of life than back in Hertfordshire. Barbara and Bernard were lovely to us and I hankered to move. Finally Ron agreed, although he found changing schools a wrench. I have never regretted this move, especially as the M25 now links with the M1 in our former "village"!

It was unbelievable to find ourselves in such spacious surroundings. We had nearly two acres of land (later acquiring another small field with stream), and a three-storey "longhouse" (four rooms end-to-end on each floor). A bus stopped in the lane outside to take our four oldest children to a small school three miles away. Son Stephen was a toddler when we moved to the "real" country. Later, our two youngest daughters were born in Suffolk. To be sure, the house was a little spartan, full of draughts and makeshift corners, and we could not at first afford carpets. But, we had SPACE!

"Holidays" remained rare events, and usually consisted of visits to relatives. As these were scattered from Devon to Yorkshire, and from Surrey to the Trent and Mersey Canal in Cheshire, we had some fun. We were rather an embarrassment to hosts, there were just too many of us. But often two or three children would go alone, sometimes by train, to distant places. Aunts, uncles and grandparents took them to the Norfolk coast, Anglesey, Yorkshire, and even to Scotland. As they entered secondary school there were Scout camps, foreign exchanges, and occasional "school holidays" away from Suffolk – to the Peak District, to the coast, even once or twice to France.

However we still did not have many "family" holidays. An added difficulty (apart from the expense) was, the fact that we usually owned at least one house cow, plus hens, ducks, geese, rabbits, the occasional goat, a dog and at least one cat! We also owned a wicked and manipulative fat grey pony for eleven years. Although two or three children could sit on his broad back one behind the other, Uncle Tom Cobley style, as he grazed the "lawn", once taken outside our gates he could become a fiend, throwing riders off and galloping over the hills and far away. We loved him, but he was a liability. Our cows too (except one or two docile doe-eyed Jerseys) also tended to be on the wild side. The last two we acquired had not been de-horned in their youth and used their lethal curved headgear to get their own way. They egged each other on into mischief –

once, to our amazement, they jumped clean over a neighbour's high-hedge-and-ditch boundary, one after the other. I had never previously believed in "the cow that jumped over the moon!" I rushed into the neighbours' garden wielding a broom, to keep the marauding beasts away from the precious greenhouse, only to be met at the back door by the startled son of the house, wearing only a bath towel! Life was never without incident. At the time our behaviour did not seem too outlandish since other neighbours owned goats, or a few pigs or cows, or a similarly unruly pony, and theirs too would suddenly appear in our rose-beds or vegetable patch.

Today, thirty-two years on, our once-rural village is increasingly suburban and prosperous in character. Many folk with large gardens such as ours have "grown" clusters of new executive homes; old wooden barns have become luxury dwellings; the dreaded BSE and foot-and-mouth disease have seen the end of the last dairy and fattening herds. The village still has fields of sheep, plenty of poultry in back gardens and a few goats. But the only pigs are housed away from sight, in their thousands, in huge modern buildings. We can tell they are there by the smell when the wind is in the wrong quarter! Likewise, enormous chicken factories grace one corner of the village, and huge lorries transport these hapless creatures to the slaughter.

So, we love our Suffolk village and friends, but thirty-two years have seen some changes and we are nostalgic for the old days (perhaps it's our age!).

Back to the subject of holidays. The most we achieved as a family was one week in a bungalow right on the remote stony Suffolk coast (luckily, a ramshackle place with tacked-on wooden "bathroom" and furniture straight out of the Twenties), into which we managed to cram an illegal thirteen people (some very small); and a week in a caravan near Lowestoft, into which we once again furtively sneaked more children than there were beds.

Ron was the only wage-earner. I occasionally joined potato-

or fruit-picking gangs, worked as a home tutor to a boy with long-term injury, and did short-time supply in small local schools who were tolerant enough to accept me even when accompanied by a toddler. I would not farm my children out and work full time; anyway I could never have coped. In 1978 our youngest daughter started school, and our eldest son simultaneously left for university. That Autumn I at last went back to teaching and the lean years were over.

This meant "proper" family holidays were at last a possibility – just in time, as the family were beginning to leave home! Our first adventure was to a camp-site at Valras Plage, on the north-west coast of the Mediterranean. We crammed ten of us into our van, which had no side windows, and front seats only (driver plus two passengers). There were eight children, since a schoolfriend accompanied daughter Anne. Anne comes between two pairs of boys in the line-up, and wanted the company of a girl her own age. Fortunately, tents and all cooking equipment were provided on site so we only needed sleeping bags, clothes and toilet items. Just the same it was an uncomfortable scramble for the passengers in the back, with a definite resemblance to sardines in a tin! We had with us groundsheets and a very small tent to make wayside stops more possible.

On the third afternoon, the van shuddered to a halt on the campsite. This was a canvas slum, redeemed by constant sunshine and the friendly ambience. Daily, we trekked across a vast sun-baked salt flat to the beach. Once there, we were accosted by dark gentlemen from the north coasts of Africa, selling sweets, food and delightful necklaces made from pieces of shell. These soft-spoken entrepreneurs left their families at home and came to France for the lucrative summer season.

Some of our party had a go at wind-surfing. From "our" beach we could see the protruding hulk of a large wreck. Sinister jagged fragments jutted out at wayward angles. Naturally, this wreck was a magnet to our lads, who insisted on trying to circle it whatever the wind direction might be. As the boys disappeared rapidly towards the horizon, the beach guards would set out grumbling in their motor boat, to tow them back. I kept a low profile, hoping no one would connect me with all these goings-on.

As parents, we had other anxious moments. The countryside was wild, dry and barren-looking, and farming consisted of vineyards and maize fields among stony open plains on which sturdy black cattle were fattened. These were tended by "cowboys" on horseback. Houses were rough square blocks around which people were rarely visible. In the daytime shutters were tightly closed to keep out the heat and it was difficult to tell which were inhabited.

One day the two older girls announced they were going off for a walk. Long blond hair loose around their shoulders and clad only in bikinis, they were soon out of sight. They were gone a long time and we started to worry. We would have worried much more if we had known what was happening. They were seventeen years old, and (as far as we knew) fairly naive.

Hours later they returned and recounted their adventure. They had met two cowhands on horseback, and got talking. There must have been a language difficulty! The girls' understanding was that they were being offered a ride on the horses, if they went with the men. I really don't know what the men thought! However they walked a long way to a shambling stone farmhouse. Going inside, they saw a huge room crowded with French women of various ages, busy (of course) preparing a vast meal on a bare wooden table that took up most of the floor area. Later more swarthy men appeared. No one offered the girls a ride on a horse. They felt they were being scrutinised by the women; rather less-than-friendly sidelong glances came their way. Eventually, drinks and plates of steaming savoury stew were offered. Even so, the girls sensed that the welcome was not universal! Not knowing quite what to do or say next, they eventually made awkward gestures and mumblings of thank you and farewell, and started the long trek home over the parched landscape. They were exhausted and not at all sure what our reaction would be. We were just greatly relieved to have them back with us, safe and sound.

In the evenings on the crowded campsite, stocky powerful men would appear and fry fresh sardines over portable charcoal grills. We had to buy some. They were crisp and hot and very heavily sprinkled with herbs we could not identify.

We visited various towns during this trip and particularly liked Béziers. Around every corner was some delightful surprise: steps led to tiny cobbled squares, stone archways revealed open-air cafés, and everywhere huge maples with mottled bark emerged from the tarmac to provide welcome leafy shade.

Our journey homewards took us eastwards along the coast; we were disappointed to see so much litter spoiling these so-called golden sands, and were not sorry to turn northwards up the Rhône valley. We spent a few days with a family in Lyon, where we shared their luxurious home. These were friends of my brother and his wife. The men had worked together in Africa. Falling into soft beds the first evening, exhausted from camping. heat and travel, none of us stirred until around ten the following day! Part of the reason was that we were not used to tight-fitting shutters. Awakening in pitch-dark rooms, we had each thought it must still be night time! We were not reluctant to accept this generous hospitality, since the previous summer the teenage son of the family had spent five weeks with us in England. He was not an easy guest; we felt he was at best a disturbed child, at worst, delinquent. Sending our own peaceable son Jim back to France to spend two weeks with this lad and his family had felt like sending a lamb among wolves.

As we neared the port, our van filled up with crates of over-ripe peaches, melons and pears, irresistible at roadside stalls. After several days on the road, these got inextricably entwined with various toothbrushes, tools, trinkets, maps, and so on. We were in a sticky mess. For some incomprehensible reason, Ron chose this journey to become unusually kind to hitch-hikers! The Customs people took one horrified look inside our battered van, were told there were ten of us, and hastily waved us through. We were truly innocents abroad; I will never forget the look of incredulity on son David's face as he read aloud the customs notice declaring that each passenger was allowed one litre of toilet water tax-free. "Toilet water?" he repeated in bewilderment – "what do they mean, toilet water?" He was (and remains) unacquainted with the finer points of skin and body beautification.

That was our first family trip to France. We never again succeeded in taking all the family. During the 1980s my brother was keen for us to admire and use his farmhouse near Bordeaux. During these visits we would investigate the enormous wood-and-concrete cider-making structure in the outhouse, gaze at the rickety stone *pigeonnier* tower, and admire the stables, in which each stall had a beautifully carved aperture of bleached white wood to accommodate the stocky head and neck of each tired horse bent to the trough. We would wander in the whispering dry grasses behind the house where cicadas made endless music. From these meadows I once carried home a green praying mantis wrapped in a leaf. We visited many times, sometimes to stay and help a little, sometimes just passing through. On our first visit, sons David and Tom played an early-morning game of tennis which left them badly roasted and uncomfortable for many days – we just were not used to the strength of the sun's rays. On a later trip, Juliet, aged nine, spent a few days in a darkened room for the same reason, mildly delirious and heard to moan "I'm too young to die!" (Perhaps we are just slow learners).

To alleviate the unforgiving blaze of mid-day heat, we would visit a local lake, Castel-Gaillard, where we could swim, or hire pedaloes, or demonstrate that we were old hands at wind-surfing. Today this lake boasts more sophisticated tourist attractions such as giant flumes. Then as now, you can ride around the shores on hired ponies, across rough slopes where butterflies flock to the scented wild thyme and marjoram, and flag irises flourish in the low marshes. I think this is a man-

Windsurfing, lac Castel-Gaillard

made lake. It certainly adds to the all-round attractions of the area.

We loved the countryside around Bordeaux. We marvelled at the rock-dwellings precariously perched on high cliffsides at Castelmoron. I wondered how on earth anyone safely reared children in such a situation. We visited many untouched bastide towns, carefully preserved by the French from unsympathetic development (I wish we could achieve the same in English historic towns). Best of all, we loved Monpazier, high up in the wooded hills, bedecked with glorious geraniums and cannas on every step and balcony. The market square or *place* was a dream, surrounded on all sides by ancient stone archways and arcades. We also loved the *château* at Duras. What an eye for breathtaking romanticism these long-ago builders possessed.

During the late 1980s, we were able to take life more easily as we travelled, partly because we were fewer in number, and partly because hospitality was available to us in several dis-

Chinon chateau and town – Ruth's flat in ornate house, front right

tricts. Ron is one of eleven children, born and brought up in a
mining village near Doncaster. Two of his sisters spent time in
France – Edith, during training to become a teacher of French,
and Ruth (also a teacher) due to involvement with twinning
between Tiverton in Devon, and Chinon in the Loire. Ruth
loved the valley and town of Chinon so much that she took
early retirement and found rented accommodation in Chinon.
For several years she lived beside the river Vienne, in a superb
second-floor apartment within an ornate and spacious town
house. Rising up behind the buildings of this historic town was
the vast *château*, much of it only semi-ruin, built of almost
white stone. We could wander through lofty chambers hung
with fabulous tapestries, displaying scenes which seemed to
combine ancient mythology with epic chivalry and the exploits
of French nobility. One year, in this *château*, we stumbled upon
a portrayal of the history of town and castle, given by a talent-
ed performer with the aid of puppets. We didn't understand it
all, but were nevertheless enchanted. Another time, we arrived
after a mighty pageant had taken place; outside the castle walls

stood a life-size battering-ram, and a contraption designed to fire huge stones – a kind of monstrous catapult.

We were able to help Ruth a little by transporting furniture, and she was always delighted to see us. She had made many French friends (including an elderly count who lived in a *château*) and was eking out her pension by translating French to English for various clients. Sadly, around the time when we purchased our *fermette*, a combination of exceptionally low interest rates in England and the worst exchange rate (from the English point of view) for years, forced Ruth to return to England. She now lives near her son and grandchildren in Devon – by coincidence, near my mother. I got them together, and now Ruth gives my mother a French lesson once a week.

We also had a pad in Paris! Son Stephen had become close friends with his exchange partner Stephane. Stephane and his handsome parents had stayed with us several times in Suffolk. The small family of three appeared to dote on each other, and they were so good-looking and so well-dressed that we felt like clumsy oafs beside them. I will never forget their unfailing

Arches and arcades at Monpazier

courtesy. How unexpected to a mere Englishwoman was their greeting on that first Suffolk morning! They slept late. When they awoke I was in the garden gathering raspberries. Suddenly the visitors appeared and tenderly embraced me, planting the statutory kisses on each cheek among the fragrant raspberry rows!

Stephane's father was a plumber and the family lived in a block of flats in central Paris. They had pleaded with us to visit them, so we arranged to spend a night there during a homeward-bound journey. It was not easy locating the right sky-rise block in this area overcrowded with buildings, traffic and people. Finally, persistence was rewarded. We parked the van, and began to mount an unattractive central metal stairway. The lifts were out of order. Every landing was dank and dirty, adorned with rubbish, graffiti and other signs of vandalism. Quite frankly, we did not feel particularly safe in these surroundings. Doors were painted in drab colours, with no names, only a number. When we finally found the correct floor and uninviting door, we were half inclined to turn round and go home defeated. But *bon courage!* – we rang the bell, and the world was suddenly transformed! Seeing the friendly smiling faces, receiving kisses on both cheeks, being welcomed in – suddenly the world was bright and good again. The inside of their spacious flat was in complete contrast to the air of dereliction and decay in the public parts of the block. Every inch was gaily decorated with a great eye for detail. The rooms were perfect, with tasteful small touches, such as the pierrots hanging from the bathroom wall, and exquisite bohemian artefacts in every corner. We were made so welcome, and henceforward admired this couple even more.

Our son spent one entire summer month with these friends. They habitually took a long let on a cottage on a riverbank in the Landes, a sandy flat landscape of pine forests and meadows in south-west France. Here, the father and son would spend hours each day fishing. I have to admit that our son found this rather boring, and preferred to go on long bike rides. But they looked after him splendidly. When we drove down to pick him up in late August, we were invited to dine with them and their regular holiday neighbours. Naturally, on the menu was fish soup. We were astounded to look into our mysterious bowls of murky liquid, only to see tiny whiskery faces looking back at us! Floating in the soup were tiny crabs, cockles, mussels, langoustines and smaller shrimps, among hunks of unidentified fish-flesh, with even the occasional whole squid. How on earth were we to eat it?

Neither spoons nor knife and fork were adequate – it had to be fingers. We messed around for ages, discarding bits, sucking other bits, and generally making a display of how not to eat in public. I am sure we were in fact highly honoured to be given this great speciality!

Our son Jim also spent an exchange sojourn in Paris. His "partner" was a black Caribbean girl, a year his senior. Luckily there were younger brothers. too. He felt the family made superhuman efforts as hosts. Father was a bus driver, they lived in a tower block, money was tight. Jim was given a bed, other members of the family slept on the settee. He was given larger portions than the family at every meal, and he would feel all eyes on him as he ate, in mute desire that he should enjoy all that they struggled to do for him. It gave Jim new insight into the lives of others.

To resume the travel theme: it was now possible for us to spend a few days here, a few there, and travel in a more relaxed and civilised manner. On one occasion, we took the ferry to Cherbourg – just Ron, myself and our youngest daughters Elisabeth and Juliet. We visited Mont St. Michel, marvelling at the myriad crooked streets winding upwards towards the amazing pinnacled edifice surmounting the rocky island – so many historic corners, so many twists and turns, so many touristy entrapments, all packed into such a tiny space. We drove on to spend some time at Chinon. A few days later we descended on brother David and sister-in-law Nicole, at Bordepaille. They took us to a classical concert in a tiny fortified village. Together we walked through fields, David picked wild vine leaves, and back at the house we feasted on a mixture of herbs, spices, onions, tomatoes and minced beef. Small spoonfuls of the mixture were wrapped tightly in large vine leaves, and steamed. Nicole and David both excelled at culinary arts.

After a few days we moved on, for a week in a cottage in a small hill village in north-west Spain, able to dine under the walnut and eucalyptus trees, and watch the neighbours bring home horse-drawn cartloads of freshly cut grass to feed to the few precious cattle tethered under the wooden balconies of their homes. Then, back through the lower slopes of the Pyrenees where small pointed hay-ricks dotted the meadows, to the Dordogne where we met friends who had gone to live there permanently. Life was becoming much less arduous! I wonder why we didn't just contentedly continue with this style of holiday, but I suppose we humans always want more – particularly the unattainable!

There is one more French family holiday I must mention. From a brochure, we selected a campsite on the south-west coast of France. On the map, this appeared as a wild, unpopulated area and the distance from site to beach was small. We booked – five children, two adults. We drove down, arriving at dusk in time to pitch our tent. Now, this was a second-hand bargain, which meant that the original instructions were no longer with the tent. It has living area, porch, and three small "bedrooms" with integral groundsheet. The salesman was slick and efficient. We are surely as competent as other campers, we thought – if we watch and listen carefully, we can do it.

Well, we have erected this tent in various corners of Europe, but every time it is a nightmare and we get no better at it! To start with, different members of the family have different memories of the final shape and layout – which side does the "gable ventilation window" go? Where is the highest point supposed to be? Which is the longer dimension, front to back or side to side?

We always start with confidence, then discussions become heated, we accuse each other: someone has let go their end at the wrong moment, just when the pieces were almost forced together; or someone has bent a section, someone has hidden a section, someone has fixed the wrong bits first – it is terrible. All around us will be campers who arrived sensibly in daylight and who erected their superior-sized tents in a flash: they watch us (we imagine) with scorn. And then of course a force eight gale starts up, or the rain becomes hail and dusk falls. Somehow, we have always finally managed to get the vital parts the right way up and the right way out before we fall asleep, even if the finished product looks a little different from last time...

A camping crisis!

Of course, we have made the intelligent moves from time to time when the thing is actually standing. We have colour-coded ends that go together, using paint or sticky tape. But there are so many ends – more than there should be since some sections were originally held in sequence by long thin chains running inside the metal cylinders, and most of these

45

chains have snapped. There are not enough colours in the rainbow to colour-code all the ends, and when using a system of letters to match, we have gone right through the alphabet and had to continue with AA, BB, and so on.

On this Atlantic trip as always, the "bedrooms" finally manifested themselves and we slept well, after a supper prepared and eaten largely by touch since we were conserving torch batteries. Next morning, we leapt up ready to investigate the beach. We were joined on the well-worn track across the dunes by various scantily-clad folk – extremely scantily clad, as it turned out! Unwittingly, we had chosen a nudist beach. We were grossly over-dressed (and determined to remain so). Ron was too abashed to raise his eyes. I had a good look: mainly, because I literally don't know what some types of nude body look like – I mean, very old bodies, or very overweight bodies – and every kind was on display. Elisabeth and Juliet (aged twelve and nine) were reluctant to look directly at any of our sun-bathing or disporting neighbours. One thing that had us all smiling, however, was a chap who every day walked down to the beach in shoes, socks, tee-shirt, and baseball cap – and nothing else! He was like a kind of negative image of the usual beach gear. Exhibitionist, or what?

We enjoyed the holiday despite horrendous thunderstorms and sheet lightning. We dug deep trenches all around our tent and ended up with our own moat. We became firm friends with a Basque family. We enjoyed the dramatic Atlantic breakers. We drove inland to explore caves, grottoes and so-called troglodyte dwellings with impressive studded oak doors. But exploring the coastline to the north and to the south of us was almost an impossibility. The shoreline was backed with sand dunes and marram grass, giving way to extensive pine woods. In these shady woods stood hundreds of holiday chalets or log cabins. Out of these cabins, and out of all the campsites, emerged other folk also attempting to travel the coast road. The traffic jam was nigh on permanent and no fun in the heat. It was very much a tourist coast with prices to match. We did get as far as Arcachon to the north, and Biarritz to the south. Parts of Biarritz are a charming time warp, with elegant small hotels, giving rise to dreams of the idle rich in sports cars and casinos early in the century. We also crossed the border into Spanish hill country to feast our eyes on streets of tall wooden houses, balconies on every floor cascading with bright petunias and pelargoniums.

By the 1990s we were usually Derby and Joan. We were untrammelled and free. We could travel without a tent, since there was enough floor-space in the van for us to take a double mattress and bedding. By this time, I was beginning to assess locations with a view to possible second-home purchase. Some of the districts we had visited and liked were too far south, and too pricey, to be considered. So one Easter we set off to drive around the Brittany coast, and then inland to the Plateau de Millevaches in Central France. Brittany was lovely, but cool, windswept, and a bit too much like England climate-wise. We noticed cottages and restored towers along the coast, the cottages hunched against the salt gales, and turned inwards for shelter. Windows faced away from the sea, giving an insight into winter conditions. Walking along one of these rugged coasts, we looked down and saw a beach strewn with literally hundreds of huge unbroken clam shells. I scrambled down and collected as many as I could carry, to use in school and give to the children in my class.

Moving inland, we had a great time exploring lonely river valleys. Several times we drove down to sheltered corners along the Creuse, the Maulde, and other placid rivers deep in wooded valleys. We were quite undisturbed, only the odd fisherman was seen. We cooked bacon and eggs on a primus and brewed up tea, in perfect peace. We visited Lac de Vassivière, with its sculpture-covered island. We drove north, investigating limestone caves which had been used as homes (one was even for sale) and passing the curious flat area of woods and small lakes south-west of Rheims. Soon after this I began to study "French Property News" with fervour, knowing where my intentions for the future lay.

While on the subject of journeys, I will mention our current mad-cap journeys to and from the *fermette*. We are like a speeded-up film. At first things were leisurely; we would take time to camp on the journey. I had purchased a tiny igloo-style tent for less than twenty pounds. It was blissfully easy to erect. It was July, and being perilously short of fuel as night fell, we parked on a busy roadside verge for the night. We had tried several garages, but they were unmanned, and only holders of special cards (fuel cards for certain brands only) could use the pumps. So we settled down. Next morning, Ron was cooking bacon and eggs, on rough grass only yards from passing traffic, when I noticed for the first time a label on our little tent. It read "PLAY TENT – NOT TO BE USED DURING RAIN"! I had bought a children's garden play tent! I had to laugh, especially when, a few moments later, we suddenly realised it was our thirty-fourth wedding anniversary! Would we never grow up?

The first time we visited Pradelette together, we made several detours on our home journey. We visited marvellous cave homes in the Loire valley. Being hollowed out within soft white limestone cliffs,

Cave dwelling in the Loire valley

they were not too gloomy inside. One charming owner charged only ten francs per head to visitors. In his lofty arched chamber, one alcove held a double bed, another a comfy chesterfield, and another a grand piano! He even had windows dug through to daylight on two sides of his home. He told us that because his cave was high in the cliff, it was never damp for long – the water simply dripped on down to the lower levels. This cliff was apparently riddled with tunnels and secret passageways made and used by protagonists in long-ago conflicts. Beautiful it might be – but I would not risk money in such an "investment"!

We also visited *châteaux* and cathedrals, such as Chartres with its rose-coloured windows circling the dome-shaped interior, and its intricate carving (so much skill and artistry!) adorning every inch of the outer wall. But on current journeys, we visit no more. We rush – almost in ever-decreasing circles, I fear. We avoid Paris and the dreaded *Peripherique*. It was a nightmare by day, so we had a second try at night. This was even worse! The traffic was more solid than ever, and we came off before our scheduled exit in order to buy fuel and visit conveniences. The garage was open, but the conveniences were closed, apparently because they were the haunt of drug-dealers and users. To make matters worse, there seemed to be no way of getting back onto the *Peripherique*. We had to negotiate a new route through Versailles.

While on the subject of French roads and French drivers, I must say that according to our experiences, the French do not deserve their reputation for wild and outrageous driving. They are, on the whole, at least as courteous and law-abiding as drivers in Britain. Now and again we have the odd hair-raising experience however. The first occurred as we drove through a large town in central France, our van crammed with bodies and camping gear. Unwittingly, we enraged the driver of a huge articulated lorry. I'm not sure what our sin was – probably, not knowing the town layout, we changed lanes perilously near some junction. Whatever we did, it was obviously a heinous crime to this man, who sounded his horn with violence while glaring across the traffic at us. We tried to get away but somehow he was alongside us at every hold-up through this town centre, squeezing us almost onto the pavement, swooping in front of us, hooting and glowering. Eventually we rushed away at traffic lights and zoomed along the next stretch of open countryside, nervously wiping our brows and glancing behind us. We were safe! We began to relax. Then we entered another town – more hold-ups. At the next junction, with a screech of brakes and heavy wheels, this lorry driver from hell was alongside us again, still hooting, still glowering. We were terrified. We escaped by suddenly swooping down a side road. It didn't matter where we ended up so long as it was not under his enormous wheels!

Another time, we were driving in Lot and Garonne country, along a wooded, peaceful main route. Without warning, a shiny new car emerged at speed from a minor road to our right, without even slowing down. Ron braked and swerved, narrowly avoiding a collision. But all was not well with our passengers in the back. Jim had been stretched out snoozing on the floor of the van, and the jolt had sent him spinning along the metal floor, badly jarring his wrist as it hit the fixings of the seats. He does not usually make a fuss and was obviously in considerable pain.

Not sure what injury he had suffered, we decided to seek medical aid. After one or two abortive attempts to find a doctor in the next small towns, hopefully at an open surgery, we decided the best plan was to find a hospital casualty department. We therefore drove about twenty miles to the town of Dax and arrived outside the hospital. By this time, Jim felt much more comfortable, but having spent so long seeking aid we wanted at least to be sure that no bones were broken.

The family stayed in the van. Jim and I entered the hospital, hoping to explain ourselves. But my French (regarded as the best in the family) was not up to the job! Jim has quite a large, but handsome, nose, and had spent hours in the sun.

Therefore, the nose was lobster-coloured and peeling. Medics and nurses, one by one, seemed rivetted by this nose. They peered at it from every angle, concerned and fascinated. We kept exclaiming and gesturing, pointing at the swollen wrist and crying: *"Non, non, pas le nez! Le nez est toujours comme ça. C'est le bras, seulement le bras est blessé!"*

By the time we convinced the experts that the arm and wrist were the problem areas, Jim and I were helpless with laughter. The mad situation felt like a dream in which you simply cannot get through to other people. Jim was obviously feeling much better. The kindly nurses finally agreed to x-ray the wrist and arm, and bandage it. No bones were broken, rest was advised.

At home some weeks later, we received a bill for this treatment (despite having the correct Form E111 with us) for which I had to obtain a bank draft in French francs to post to the French authorities.

I must admit that the bad driving we experience in France is usually our own! One hazard, which occurs regularly, is our inability to remember, first thing in the morning, that we must drive on the right. We wake up at Pradelette, set off to buy the breakfast *pain* in the nearby small town, and are usually the only vehicle on the road. So there is nothing to remind us; suddenly one of us will shout (as we near a blind bend or a hilltop): "Help, we're on the wrong side of the road – move over, quick, before we meet anything!"

We had another lucky escape one spring morning near Jonzac. We had spent a night with our son and his girl-friend, who were temporarily living in that area of France. We rounded a corner in bright sunshine, only to find ourselves skidding wildly from side to side, bumping banks and walls and totally out of control. Finally stopping, we saw that the van was rolling on large hailstones. They were about six inches deep on the road, deeper still in the nooks and crannies where the wind had heaped them. Getting out to walk around and calm our nerves, we discovered that this deep swathe of hailstones only extended about a quarter of a mile in each direction. Elsewhere the road was entirely dry and clear. We had driven blithely onto the scene, in the wake of a small but intense freak hailstorm.

How many more long and hazardous journeys will we undertake in pursuit of our dream, I wonder? We are getting rather long in the tooth for arduous adventures on the road.

I keep threatening to book the ferry tickets myself and arrange at least one night in a hotel each way, as befits our age. Maybe one day we won't need to take tools, furniture or food, maybe we will fly over. Meanwhile, I'm not going to nag as I am so pleased Ron has willingly shared this near-obsession of mine and we're happily meeting each challenge together.

Now, on with the story of our *fermette* and its restoration! *"Bon courage, mes amis!"*

8

REALITY DAWNS

AS THE rash new owner of a near-derelict stone dwelling I had very little idea what restoration would involve. It did not seem fair to expect Ron to undertake the work, and I naively thought I could get builders to do what was needed, bit by bit, as I could afford it. Accordingly, we took a builder friend of ours with us one October, and aided by his knowledge tackled various tidying-up and repair work. He was fascinated but a little horrified by the state of the *fermette*. Being interested in old places and wanting experience on the Continent, he agreed to return with a friend the following Spring. So in March, he set off armed with a list of priorities and a van full of tools and food.

To my utter dismay, he returned four days later, saying the house was too cold, too uncomfortable and dusty, and most importantly, there was no water so he couldn't mix cement or mortar. I just didn't want to believe what I was hearing, but we later discovered the reason for the complete lack of water and the weather forecast confirmed that all central France was deep in snow.

I searched the pages of "French Property News" and discovered an English builder living in France who specialised in restorations. He agreed to meet us at the *fermette* in May. I was once again full of hope. The meeting went well and I thought I had explained my wishes clearly. One of the first tasks was to repair holes in the bedroom walls and re-point between the stones, then install a toilet and shower in a section of the bedroom divided from the main area by a huge low beam which formed an essential part of the roof structure. We parted with optimism.

Some months later I received detailed plans from this builder. They were for the bedroom and were amazingly complex. He planned a split-level floor, steps to a higher-level mezzanine area, steps down to the shower – the whole would result in several small poky rooms. I wrote what I felt was a polite and reasonable letter, thanking him for his plans. I said that I loved the simple spaciousness of the rooms, and preferred the bedroom to retain its original character and not be divided up as in his plan.

In response to this I received an alarmingly irate letter written in capitals. The writing deeply scored the paper suggesting extreme anger. The gist was that not everyone can produce plans and do restorations and he did not want to carry out any of my instructions unless I employed a good architect to validate them, thank you.

Since I could barely afford a jobbing builder, let alone an architect, I wrote back, trying to sound grateful and conciliatory. I said I was sorry to have involved him in work that led nowhere, but we had decided to do the work ourselves. Back to square one!

After this we slowly began to tackle quite major work and learned as we went along. Some jobs were beyond us so we had to call in experts. Thus Didier, living three miles from the *fermette*, put in two French windows (of course!) and three small casements, all of which we acquired in England and carried over to France in the van. One of these originally came from the old school in our Suffolk village and was given to Ron for use as a garden frame. I spotted it in the garden and suggested it would look just right on the north side of the *fermette*. Hey presto! It was stripped, repaired, stained, and reborn to a new life across the Channel. Didier cut stone to surround these new windows and doors and they look superb.

Didier also installed our septic tank drainage. I was struggling with both the language and the requirements of the official permit for this work: "Help, it says here I've got to draw a plan of all existing streams and ditches on and around our land, including underground ones! How do I know where they are?"

"There's water running all over the place after rain, some of it seems to run under the house, and I'm sure most of that smelly ditch the other side of the track runs over to our side!"

"Let's ask Didier what to do!"

Didier took one look at our worried faces, smiled serenely, and drove us to the local Mairie. Here, he greeted the Deputy Mayor (an attractive young woman) who apparently did just about all the routine work. Obviously she was Didier's lifelong friend and neighbour. A few mysterious marks were made on the *permis*, which was duly signed with a flourish and smiles all round. Problem over!

But things did not always run so smoothly. Often it has been a case of two steps forward, one step back (or even one step forward and two back). For example, we wanted to remove the old garden wall, soil, ivy and tree roots, that made the long

Digging the terrasse with some neighbourly help

north wall of the house so damp and ruinous. One July, we dug away with spades and wheelbarrow, burning roots and sorting stones. Our friendly Swiss neighbour Simone, with her children Helene, Pauline and Claude, were delighted to have the topsoil for their flower garden. In a week, we had cleared half the distance, but it was time to return to England and there was about thirty-five feet more to do. Someone recommended a man with a mechanical digger, living in a nearby hill village.

We never met this man, receiving his bill by post in England. We paid without seeing the results of his efforts. He it was who dug clean through the mains water pipe, breaking it and leaving it pointing skywards from a mountain of mixed rubble at one end of the garden. That was why our builder friend found no water on his March visit.

If this had happened to us in England we would have complained and demanded compensation. But we did not want to damage the *entente cordiale*, we did not want to be known as that awkward English couple; besides, complaining is much more difficult in a foreign language! So we meekly paid for repairs to pipes, and re-connection to the mains. Not cheap.

Another builder (delivered to our door by his wife, since he had been convicted of drink driving) was glad to sit imbibing our wine and telling us his various exploits, before agreeing to fit four Velux roof lights on the south side of our long roof. He was very likeable, reminding me of many a mischievous little schoolboy. We found ourselves laughing wildly as he recounted how he had once set his magnificent curled moustache on fire while lighting a cigarette as he drove. He was a natural comic; his wry features and flamboyant gestures told the whole story even where the words were too quick for us.

But on our next visit to France, where was our row of four Veluxes? They were at each end of the building, two on the south side and two on the north! This was the easy option, as there was no first floor to the middle sections of the *fermette*. Putting the windows in a row on the south side, as requested, would have been much more difficult, requiring roof ladders.

I pointed out that our *permis* was for roof lights on the south side only. He waved his hands dismissively, saying not to worry, the Mayor was a member of the *chasse* of which he himself was chief. We later learned the two were great drinking buddies.

Once again, like a fool, I paid up. We bought two more Veluxes and asked for them to be installed to complete the row along the south side. Our friend agreed, but did nothing. A year later, I sought him out in his village. His was the last of four small villages reached by a long lane through woods, and was a real hideout as none of the names of these villages

A 'Veluxes' discussion

appeared on any signs. But he was out. His distraught young wife chatted to us. Then a car drove up, a young man got out and presented the wife with the car keys, explaining (as far as I could make out) that he and Monsieur had been driving towards home together, when all of a sudden our friend the builder had disappeared! There one minute, gone the next – "*Il est disparu!*" repeated his apparently baffled friend. The wife shrugged her shoulders with resignation. I don't think it was the first time her husband had thought it best to disappear. We left in search of another builder!

Sometimes our own efforts went badly awry. The winter after my husband had mended the rotten bedroom floor, five or six tiles again blew off the roof, resulting in a sodden and dangerous bedroom floor, which we strengthened with thick composition board. Later, Ron placed our longest ladder

"Our fitted kitchen"

against the roof intending to climb up and replace tiles. At this moment, a jovial man in a panama hat came out of our neighbours' house to see what was going on. (I think they had been celebrating, he was very happy!) We pointed to our missing tiles. As if giving a demonstration to very slow-witted folk, he lurched up our ladder and started removing more tiles from our roof with gay abandon, to show how easy it was. He seemed disappointed when we shouted *"Non, non!"* He was so keen to help.

The problem with tiles being blown off every winter was solved when we purchased some right-angled tiles specially made for gable ends. With these firmly nailed in place, all stayed intact. This was not always true of the stones, however. One summer we installed a smart toilet with stylish green porcelain seat cover and cistern. On our next visit, we discovered a hunk of granite had fallen from the top of the wall (these walls are almost dry-stone) and crashed on to cistern and seat. Another patch-up job. We tried not to become disheartened.

We managed to think positive most of the time, to put right what went wrong and look on the bright side. But on our first visit of the year 2000 I came near to giving up. We arrived to find holes in the terracotta tiles of the *grenier* floor, the result of stones dislodged from the high walls during the spectacular storms of the last days of 1999. The roof of the *grenier*, a huge structure, was wobbling in the breeze. Wind had got in at the gable end and lifted the whole roof, widening the angle of the timbers at its peak so the rafters no longer fitted the slots at the top of the wall. To make matters worse, an owl had taken up residence in the bedroom of the house, leaving nauseous greasy curls of stinking excrement everywhere – at least thirty nasty little heaps. Uneaten prey adorned the shower area – a dried out and flattened mole, and feathers everywhere. To add to our distress, Ron turned the water back on (we drain the system for winter) forgetting that last Autumn he had undone terminal isolating taps so no water could remain to freeze. So water ran through the floors.

I was very near tears. For the very first time, I wanted to give up. "We'll have to sell it, it's all too difficult!" I wailed. I'm sure Ron has secretly had this same thought many times. But he comforted me, saying: "Don't decide now, it will all seem better in the morning". And he was right.

9

HOME COMFORTS

THERE were many unknowns about our first visit as owners. Would we be able to get into all the rooms? And had the previous owner left any furniture? Certainly there had been heaps of unidentified objects in the stable when we first viewed the *fermette* – just visible through a tiny window. If any remained, would this be blessing or problem?

It was a relief to find no soggy mattresses! We had one comfy leather-covered armchair. Of all the horse-related gear, only one cart horse harness bit remained. We hung this ceremonially above the concrete feeding trough. We also had a wooden manger and hay-rack.

One huge heavy cupboard lay sideways against a wall, among various old shutters, doors, latches and iron hinges. We unearthed various curiously-shaped pieces of curved varnished wood. Many a fascinating hour was spent turning the pieces this way and that, like an enormous three-dimensional puzzle. We learned later from Didier, our builder, that they were the remains of a dismantled Creusoise box-bed. He has one in his son's bedroom.

One day, we vowed, this bed would be re-assembled, given a mattress, and polished up to grace one of the bedrooms. Chris (father-in-law of our eldest son) produced intricate drawings and plans for this future feat. For the moment, however, we turned our attention to the cupboard.

The first tasks were obvious – dust, de-cobweb, treat for woodworm (fifty years too late!) and set our antique cupboard upright. This required as many stalwart bodies as we could find, working as a team. We took some amazing photos of well-

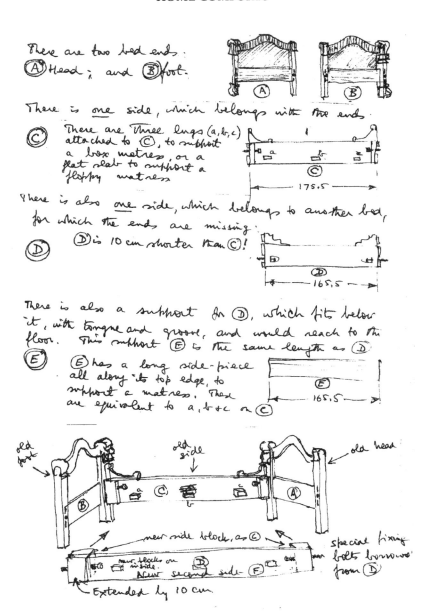

There are two bed ends.
(A) Head; and (B) foot.

There is one side, which belongs with the ends.

(C) There are three lugs (a, b, c) attached to (C), to support a box matress, or a flat slab to support a floppy matress

175.5

There is also one side, which belongs to another bed, for which the ends are missing.

(D) (D) is 10 cm shorter than (C)!

165.5

There is also a support for (D), which fits below it, with tongue and groove, and would reach to the floor. This support (E) is the same length as (D).

(E) (E) has a long side-piece all along its top edge, to support a matress. These are equivalent to a, b + c on (C)

165.5

old foot old side old head

(B) (A)

new side block, as (C)
new blocks on inside.
New second side (F)
special fixing bolts borrowed from (D)
Extended by 10 cm.

Diagrams of Creusoise bed by Chris Taylor

Allez-oop! Moving "le grand vieux placard".

nourished thighs and backsides in recording this epic event! Next, we had to make shelves. On these went all our bits and pieces of china and the stable immediately looked more homely.

Our battered van is costly on the ferry, but has great advantages over a car. Over the next few years we travelled surrounded by tools, strimmer, boxes of food, small trees, and a host of objects discarded by friends and family and thrown our way. We often speculated on the reaction should the customs men decide to search our van – I'd like to see the looks of disbelief as beds, tables, chairs, lawn-mower, curtain-poles, toilets, basins – and yes, even a kitchen sink! – were unearthed from the mysterious bowels of the vehicle. Strangely, we have never been searched. I suppose we look too simple and naive to be suspect (surely not too old?).

Once, we were asked whether we had any weapons with us! We replied doubtfully in the negative, while wondering whether garden shears, crowbar and sledge-hammer qualified.

We have furnished our house at no expense. I did not want to fill the house with new goods since no doors were locked and some will not even close properly. And I did not want the *fermette* to become a source of anxiety during the winter months when we do not visit. Local people register amazement and disbelief when we ask if our property is likely to be at risk – no crimes occur in this neighbourhood and all our good neighbours keep an eye on things for us. I am glad I didn't fall for a cottage with no neighbours, we would have missed so much pleasure and friendship.

Once people knew we wanted household gear, an astonishing variety of offerings came our way. We received bedding as well as beds, curtains, cushions, colourful mats for the stone floors, saucepans, china, cutlery – you name it, we have it! So we have an interesting assortment of not-exactly co-ordinated furnishings. Many have a history attached, such as the four leather-seated dining chairs from my parents' home, bringing back warm memories of very early childhood when I was fascinated by the way the seats lifted out. There is a slightly "Twenties" air about the rooms, as we have such items as tea trolleys with barley-twist legs, and hefty scrolled sideboards. We have a desk and table from Linda's husband's music shop which she tearfully cleared out after he had died. We have delicately-turned cottage chairs which were in a bus which daughter Juliet bought in order to travel the continent hippie-style. Daughter Anne contributed two bamboo-framed settees, four doors and a table. Son Tom came up trumps with bath and fridge. Suffolk neighbour Mary brought round a divan bed after it failed to sell at her garage-sale. Friends Graham and Elizabeth gave a corner cupboard built by Graham's father. The list goes on and on, and on – fortunately we have plenty of rooms to fill at Pradelette! But one day soon we may have to say "Thank you, but no, house full!"

I fear I am a romantic and unrealistic dreamer. Ron has his feet firmly on the ground. So there were early tensions as when he bought an electric water-heater to go above the sink. To me, it was too white, too shiny, too modern, and took away from the kitchen that feeling of having stepped back in time into an earlier age. Gradually I bowed to common-sense; after all, if we hoped other people would stay in the *fermette* and enjoy it, basic comforts were essential. We could not expect guests to heat water over a wood fire as we had done. In early days I "borrowed" a round water-tank from what I thought was a rubbish dump in the village. This receptacle was just large enough to sit down in for a proper wash – a little like a hip-bath. I later learned it belonged to a neighbour who used it for her cows' drinking water! She made no fuss, she simply quietly retrieved it when we were out! I am grateful for her tolerance.

The truth is, I like playing at the simple pastoral life. But looking back nostalgically in summertime is a far cry from being born to a life of inescapable drudgery. Reminders of long-ago tasks surround us: in the huge fireplace and bread oven, the shallow stone sinks, and (in larger villages) the communal *lavoirs* where clothes were beaten against worn granite stones, in icy water. Outside our front door is a water-filled deep hollow in the solid granite on which the *fermette* stands. This hollow once held timber supporting a sloping roof overhead, giving the housewife an extended covered area. Maybe here she would have chopped wood, plucked chickens, peeled vegetables – certainly she would have come out here to use the hand mill which stands in an angle of the wall. This mill is a huge cylinder of granite with a hole gouged out. Millet was poured into the smooth deep recess, pounded vigorously, then heated in milk to make a kind of gruel or porridge. I visualise small sinewy women draped in black, endlessly labouring to feed and clothe hungry families. The fire would be kept in winter and summer – endless smoke and ashes to contend with as well as floors and children to scrub clean.

What stories did they tell around the fireside? And afterwards, where did they all sleep? What disasters and ailments beset them? And how on earth did those short muscular men cut and manoeuvre enormous blocks of granite for lintels, cornerstones, flagstones?

We live in a softer age, we have choices, we have leisure time; compared to earlier lives we are spoiled and overindulged. I like to think that past inhabitants of our *fermette* also found time for fun and laughter in this place – I hope so.

10

ACHIEVEMENTS

"LOOK at those gorgeous stone stairs. They're kind of timeless somehow, aren't they?"

"Yes, and nothing's wasted – there's a super place for a dog to sleep, under the stairs."

"They look so solid – maybe we could have stone stairs inside the house as well?"

"No, that's not right for the area, the inside stairs are always wood. Perhaps we can buy second-hand..."

"But we've got all this stone lying around – and stone stairs would strengthen the place as well, wouldn't they?"

"Well, OK. Go ahead if you must; it's your problem."

Thus my big stair-building adventure began. It kept me busy for the next five years. Once we accepted that we would have to rely mostly on our own efforts at restoration, "holidays" tended to become labour camps. We constantly try to convince friends and family who stay with us in the Creuse, that just because we choose to spend our time slaving away, we don't expect them to do the same. Nevertheless, we have been vastly encouraged over the years by tremendous offers of help, expertise, and creative touches from others – like the enormous chandelier made from bits of farm machinery and carefully forged iron rods by friend Michael. This chandelier now graces our bedroom. It has never been wired up or given bulbs and shades, and serves as favourite perch for the small birds who still infiltrate the building. During electric storms we lie fascinated, staring up at it – supposing lightning struck the house, would the strike descend the wire from which the chandelier hangs and dramatically circle the rings which lie above our

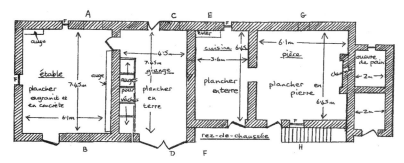

Above: the ground floor "before"

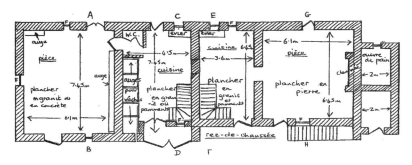

Above: the ground floor "after".
Additions are: stairs, wc, second sink, recessed new front door

heads, searching for a route downwards? Would it leap the gap to our bed and toast us?

I hope we will never know!

I am not normally a do-it-yourself addict, though of course throughout our marriage I have helped with painting and decorating. Ron on the other hand, has built shower rooms and conservatories, altered dividing walls, lowered chimneys, put in dormer windows and stairs, even created a swimming pool. I always made the coffee and the encouraging remarks.

But soon after purchasing the *fermette* I was fired with enthusiasm for trying my hand at building granite stairs.

The two halves of the *fermette* – house and farm – were divided by a wall which had at one time spanned several floors. Now, this wall was barely five feet high in places. This meant

66

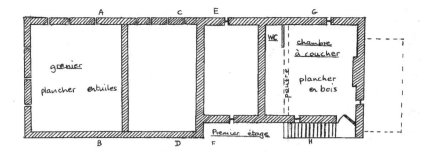

Above: the first floor "before"

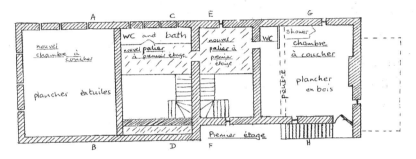

Above: the first floor "after".
Additions are: two new landings, stairs, shower room and new bathroom

that the surviving twenty-foot-high section which adjoined the big barn doors was alarmingly unsupported. Also, the outside wall beside it had a huge jagged crack.

I decided to build my stairs with a right-angle bend against these two walls. At home, I would not have dreamed of doing such a thing. Being in a remote area of France seems to liberate me and make me believe I can do anything. I am a new woman!

Anyone who has ever tried to work with rough unshaped stone knows how hard it is. Any normal person would gain a little experience on something simple, like a plain wall, before rushing in to build stairs. But fools rush in...!

Not waiting always to find the "right" stone, nor to chip the stone to shape, I got to work. I created under-stair cupboards,

One of my granite staircases, leading up to the new landing

and tried to give a graceful curve to the first few steps. The whole was held together with large amounts of cement mortar which I learned to mix, straight onto the earth floor. I was thrilled that my work actually did seem to resemble steps, even though I found it virtually impossible to keep all faces correctly horizontal or vertical. I was quite disconcerted when showing them off to my brother to hear, not praise, but: "Haven't you heard of spirit-levels and plumb lines?"

How mundane!

He was right, of course. But undeterred, I built a second staircase. We soon possessed a flight each side of the central dividing wall. Certainly the new stairs served to strengthen and reinforce the existing walls. But they had a certain eccentricity, in that they led nowhere. There was no first floor in this part of the building. You could go up one set of stairs, cross the central wall, and come down the others! I felt like the rich man in "Fiddler on the Roof". Visitors (especially French ones) tried hard to be polite, but you could see their puzzlement.

Meanwhile, Ron started his *terrasse* and new retaining garden wall. He created a shower room, which grew and grew, projecting into the big bedroom rather like the prow of the Queen Mary. He reinforced doorways, put in a downstairs loo, fitted sinks and basins with all the associated plumbing. He put in window frames and glass, and curtain rails.

68

All this building has of course necessitated frequent visits to the local builders' yard. Patron M. Gadaix is unfailingly ready to listen and watch as we do our best, through words and gestures, to explain our needs. He is dapper, alert, and as busy as an ant. There are always customers in his office, shop, and extensive yards and sheds. At one time we had trouble obtaining lime from this yard – we had brought some from England, and used it all in our various mixes, and wanted more to ensure porosity in areas where dampness would inevitably rise through walls from time to time. How could we explain? We peered at the printing on the various heaped-up sacks. None of the words seemed to suggest "lime".

"En Angleterre, on met du poudre blanc avec le ciment – avez-vous un sac de poudre blanc ici, s'il vous plaît, Monsieur?"

Our pleas were not understood. We were told that Frenchmen NEVER added suspicious white powder to their mixes. Eventually we had to concede, and left with our sacks of sand and cement, a few lengthy pieces of wood protruding from the rear doors of the van.

The dictionary came to our rescue (why do we ever leave it at home?). Lime was *"chaux"*. Triumphantly we raced back to the yard – *"Deux sacs de chaux blanc, s'il vous plaît, Monsieur!"* we cried, pouncing on the correct heap within the hangar-like storage sheds. We had breakthrough – we understood each other, there were happy smiles all around and out came the fork-lift to load us up.

Buying the correct pieces of plastic pipe and junctions, s-bends etc has required a pantomime of explanation. We are allowed to wander around shop and shed until we spy the correct piece, and have had some fun searching for just the right width and length of tongue-and-groove in forgotten corners of the buildings. Once, we needed such long lengths of four-by-four (uprights for banister and landing) that the passenger in the van had to travel bent double and clutching one end of the bundle, which extended between the front seats as far as the dashboard. The other ends stuck well out at the back of the vehicle, firmly tied to the handle of the van door, with a convenient piece of red rag tucked under the rope to act as warning red flag. What a good thing we are not tidy people! Not everyone would have a length of thick blue twine (rescued from a beach where it lay entangled with seaweed) and a small pair of red pyjamas (left from the last time we conveyed jumble to the Village Hall) at their finger tips when needed!

Monsieur Gadaix and his charming staff cannot do too much for their customers. One October morning Linda and I were driving to the yard for supplies when the van began making noises of distress. The motor jerked, stopped, started, then groaned. We juddered to a halt about 500m from the yard. What had I done? Maybe I had been in the wrong gear once too often (the five forward gears are unusually close together). Linda and I climbed down from the van and gazed at it – it was parked in a bizarre manner as I had been turning a corner when it stopped. Downhearted, we trudged into the office of M. Gadaix. He rushed from behind the counter, all smiles, to shake me by the hand: *"Bonjour, Madame, ça va?"*

"Non, Monsieur, nous avons un problème. Notre camionnette est en panne – regardez, il ne marche pas..."

Monsieur jumped into action. He phoned a local garage, asking for an engineer to come immediately. He would take no money for this call, it was his pleasure. We returned to the van and stared accusingly at it. Very soon the engineer appeared and asked the problem. He climbed into the van and turned the ignition. The engine purred into life. I felt totally at a loss – why hadn't I tried this myself? Maybe I had just over-heated the engine in some way?

But the engineer was not satisfied. He asked me to follow him to the garage workshop. The van behaved perfectly. Had I just made a complete fool of myself?

In the garage, our hero produced a torch. He lifted the bonnet and peered into the oily interior. A few moments later, like a surgeon in an operating theatre, he poked inside with tweezers and brought out a section of broken black piping. The fuel

Bridging the gap with beams to create a new first floor landing

pipe was split almost in two! I could have hugged him, greasy overalls and all. Swiftly, he replaced the part, and gave us a bill which totalled about twenty-five pounds sterling. He backed the van onto the road for me, and we were back at the builders' yard after only a twenty-minute hold up. What service.

To return to the topic of restoration. Visiting family and friends treated and stained woodwork, painted the concrete-block walls, and pointed stonework. Colleagues Elizabeth and Graham visited many times to add to our electric facilities. Alan added beautiful brick window ledges, using soft rosy floor bricks given by a neighbour.

Finally, the day arrived when a group of us started to create a first floor. We had some gigantic beams (taken from the bed-room) over five metres long and very heavy. They reached eas-ily from the existing *grenier* floor over to the rebuilt central dividing wall. Tongue and groove boards went on top of these to create a new floor. At last, "Stairs One" led somewhere! A year later, we created a floor on the other side of the central wall, though this time a lot of bodging and making-do was needed to bridge the gap with the shorter ex-bedroom timbers. The result was, a much tidier ground floor, and two new upstairs areas. I was thrilled. We had access to huge new spaces.

It took me a little time to realise that we now had access also to further acres of virtually dry stone wall which was desperately in need of repair and pointing! That's for the future.

After the stairs, I set to work building a recessed front wall within the high barn doors, and Ron had the tough task of hanging two swing doors, acquired in a Suffolk junk-yard and presumably rescued from a demolished pub or men's club. These grand oak doors have small glass panes and a lot of brass extras. They look quite imposing.

Recent tasks have included patching up some rendered walls and painting with dribbly lime-wash. We experimented with red and yellow ochre (earth colours) mixed to give a light peachy-pink to take away the cold gloomy look of rooms with a great deal of exposed stone. All the best stonework, especially door and window surrounds, is left exposed. We remain humbled and awe-struck by the work of the *maçons* of the Creuse; the thought of the hours spent dressing square blocks, and the mechanics required to heave them into perfect alignment, are almost beyond belief. And I realise most of my own "stone work" is sheer vandalism!

Eight years into the project, I think even an optimist would conclude we are only about half-way finished. Living in the *fermette* is still a kind of glorified camping.

But we do not give up easily. Witness, to date we have survived forty-two years of "wedded bliss"! (Which one of us is the hero?) As our dear neighbours Nicole and Andrée have remarked when regarding our various projects with undisguised astonishment: *"Bon courage, mes amis!"*

11

SOAKING UP SUNSHINE

"HEY, wake up! Come on, wake up and turn over – time to do the other side!"

Grunts and groans from the lightly lobster-tinted body spread-eagled on the grass – he's too far gone to move.

"OK then, I'll just cover you up with these two big towels - and there's a straw hat to go over your face – don't push it off, you need it!"

The shade from the trees behind us has moved as time slips by towards evening. As mentioned earlier, occasionally members of the family have suffered from sunstroke and sunburn. I'm becoming quite wise about such things as the hazards of unaccustomed strong sunshine on pale northern bodies. Our dear son Tom had a particularly nasty experience of this when in his teens. On the first morning of our holiday he leaped out of bed and went off to play tennis, clad in the briefest of garments. For many days afterwards, he could be spotted lurking in the shadows, heavily draped in loose flowing garments, like some shifty sheikh on the run from Interpol. Moving was painful – skin touching skin, or touching cotton sheets, or even in contact with the lightest of shirts, all were painful, and his holiday enjoyment was sadly curtailed.

Of course this kind of mishap does not only happen to those lazing on the sand or playing games in the sunshine. Heavy bodies slumped outdoors on easy chairs after a busy morning spent mixing concrete are just as vulnerable! We now have lovely sitting areas on the north, west and south sides of the *fermette*. This means we can either spend our day chasing the sun, or avoiding it, depending on season and weather!

I myself love the sun, and have the leathery wrinkles to prove it. During our first years of ownership, when we had no proper tap or sink, I would enjoy preparing vegetables, washing up, and hand-washing clothes and towels, outside in the sun. A large smooth block of granite rests on the grass just outside our stable door, which faces south. Here I would sit, revelling in the warm rays and in no hurry to finish my chores. Clean plates and cutlery would be laid out on tea towels to dry themselves in the sun. I still tend to work out here when the weather is right, even after the advent of a sink with running hot water.

We still have no washing machine, and the proud results of my labours (never bright or white like the telly ads) are pegged on a piece of binder-twine tied between trees, to dance in the wind and bleach in the lovely sunshine. Brought indoors to be carefully folded, the cloth smells nostalgically of fresh air and freedom.

At the mention of holidays, most families immediately think of sun, sea and sand. We can manage sun, water and sand quite easily in the Creuse! Some days we like to stop giving an imitation of the twelve labours of Hercules, and head for some delightful spot where we can be thoroughly lazy, and pop in and out of the water if and when we feel like it. So where do we go?

During the first few years of ownership, we scoured maps and tourist brochures for lakes or rivers large enough and deep enough to swim in. Our first discovery that fitted this bill was "Pays des Trois Lacs" (land of the three lakes), lying about fourteen miles west of Pradelette (depending on how many times you get lost). These "three lakes" are in fact a lengthy stretch of the River Creuse. The river valley varies greatly in width. At three of the narrower points along the river bed, between Glénic to the south and La Celle Dunoise to the northwest, huge hydro-electric barrages have been constructed from bank to bank. Of course swimming is not permitted near these barrages, which would be highly dangerous. They are auto-

A day out at
'Pays des Trois Lacs'

matically adjusted to reduce or increase the flow of water, or dam the river totally, depending on output of the system and amount of rainfall.

The French hydro-electric system is admirable. Most larger rivers are involved, and in addition to being an excellent source of power without resort to fossil fuels, bathing places are created to bring in tourists. (I am not so enamoured of the French network of nuclear power stations!) I remember reading somewhere about the problems caused to French country folk living in remote hilly areas near the source of the Dordogne. The traditional lifestyle of some older inhabitants has changed little – the old ways, to them, are the best ways. The coming of adjustable dams and barrages has meant that the water level is no longer predictable from season to season. Those using the river water for their own domestic and farming needs may run into unexpected difficulty. More of this later.

The Creuse in this district flows through deep, steep-sided gorges. Lanes are tiny and devious. We have discovered that the fact that a lane is descending as it twists, does not necessarily mean we are almost at the river. The lane may dip steeply only to rise up again around the next corner. Sometimes we proceed in a series of surprised jerks. On one never-to-be-forgotten occasion, our friend and neighbour Andrée was travelling with us in our dilapidated van. She was sitting in a rear seat, since the step up to the front row of seats is too high for Andrée to climb. She seemed a little nervous at the unaccustomed terrain and motion, and held on tightly. At one particularly unexpected rush forward she must have grabbed onto her seat, inadvertently pulling a lever. Suddenly, her seat shot backwards, sliding right off its metal runners to settle, back horizontal and seat vertical, on the floor of the van. We were horrified. Andrée lay scuppered like a turned turtle, her chubby little legs projecting skywards from her blue-flowered dress. We know she already suffers from *mal aux genoux* (painfully stiff knees). What injury had our guest suffered?

Miraculously, she was quite unhurt, though a little bruised and shaken. We brushed her down, patted her into shape, re-assembled her seat and re-united her with it, to the accompaniment of many a *"Ça va..! N'est pas grave, mes amis!"* What a dear brave little lady! Dignity restored, she managed to laugh with us, and with great care we conveyed her safely home, while apologising profusely in our best French. Our van has never, before or since, played such a trick on any other fellow traveller.

To resume the account of our journeys to the lakes; patience is always finally rewarded. But a good map reader is definitely an asset! In this way, we have discovered many riversides, rocky cliffs, and sandy coves over the years, but cannot always find the same spot twice. Initially, many sections of riverside seemed peaceful and unspoilt, and we would wander beside the meandering or fast-flowing water hearing only birdsong, the splash of coots or moorhens, or the plop of fish. Blackened half-submerged fallen tree trunks gave an Amazonian hint of lurking alligators. We were usually the only intrepid swimmers.

Enjoying la Grande Creuse

Year by year since then, more "Fishing Only" zones and clusters of wooden chalets have appeared; but this stretch of river valley remains mainly remote and delightfully natural.

Of course some stretches of water have long been tourist traps, and there are areas of beach, the sand thoughtfully imported for sunbathers and the sand-castle brigade. This sand is regularly shovelled up towards the banks, smoothed out, and replenished. There are swings and slides, supervised bathing areas, boats for hire, snack bars and craft shops – even archery and beach ponies in some locations. However the charm and freedom remain – you may sit on a "supervised" beach, and see on the opposite bank four hundred or so yards away, unsupervised wild youngsters daring to dive into the deep dark water from steep rugged cliffs, accompanied by shouts and shrieks of fear and laughter.

We have visited La Celle-Dunoise, Lavaud (there are two!), Cessac, le Bourg-d'Hem, Guémontel, Le Vignaud, Jupille, Anzême (which boasts a waterfall, the "Cascade des Moulines"), Chambon, Péchadoire and other tiny hamlets nestling along the shores. Glénic boasts a stupendous towering stone viaduct, now closed to traffic. Lying parallel a hundred or so yards away is the new bridge. Several miles downstream near Anzême, another bridge spans the torrent. This old granite-built bridge goes by the name "Pont du Diable", or the Devil's Bridge. Behind this name lies a fascinating legend, variations of which are to be found all over France. This is the story:

An ancient stone watermill stood on the banks of the Creuse. The miller lamented the fact that crossing from one bank to the other was a trial, since there was no bridge. One day a mysterious rider approached the miller's daughter who (like every miller's daughter!) was exceptionally beautiful. He said "I am the Devil, and I can easily build a bridge here, across this river by your father's mill, in one night. But I do so on condition that you accept my bargain: if I finish the work before the cock crows, you will belong to me. If, on the other hand, dawn should break before the bridge is completed, you will be free. But in either case, I will do a good job and give you an excellent bridge."

Well, the girl did not believe even the Devil himself could create a strong bridge over the rushing waters in a single night. So she gladly agreed to the bargain, and received from her unlikely suitor a magnificent ring. The jewel was dazzling, shooting fire this way and that. She went home rejoicing to tell her father.

The moment night fell, the Devil set to work. He worked so well that as dawn approached there only remained three huge stones to be placed. The frightened girl, seeing herself destined to be lost to the Devil, devised a clever plan. She crept into the hen house and hid among the straw. Then she waved her left hand, causing the magical stone to sparkle brightly. Tricked by this sudden ray of light, the cockerel gave a deafening "cock-a-doodle-doo!" – just as the Devil was about to lay the last stone! Mad with rage, he vanished without bothering to set the stone in place (as you can still see today).

The miller was very happy to have got his bridge. But despite her charms, his daughter still suffered. Since she was henceforward known as "the Fiancée of the Devil", she could never find any man brave enough to become her husband. *(Legend from the writings of Jean des Ajoncs).*

Further downstream stands a bridge known as "Pont de l'Enfer", or Bridge of Hell. Nature must have seemed a wild untameable beast to peasants without access to today's machinery and technology, and it is easy to imagine the dangers faced by even the strongest, most skilful of early engineers and artisans attempting to create bridges without the aid of reinforcing iron, concrete or cranes. We often marvel at the build of local people – short but broad with huge strength in shoulders, arms and hands from generations of heavy manual labour and, for most individuals, a lifetime of physical work. Going home to cottages devoid of electric light or television, the weaving of stories around the fireside must have fostered and expanded the imagination much as horror films do today! People love to be frightened, it seems! Inventing malevolent supernatural forces that oppose our best efforts has always been a forte of the human race. So as I gaze into this particular shadowy abyss or "pit of Hell" I try to share the emotions of those country folk, permitting fingers of primeval fear to run down my spine. It is a way of sharing what has gone before. I have not yet discovered the actual legend behind this name "Bridge of Hell".

Further south, below Guéret, runs a river called "Rigole du Diable", or the Devil's Rivulet. I am told that everywhere in the Creuse, the Devil is a prime character in myths and legends. Often, the story is set on riversides, and tells how the Devil built a bridge to fool some naive miller (the usual target) into parting with his daughter. Other local legends date from pre-Christian eras when gods both evil and benign were revered in the countryside. Some focus, not on rivers and lakes, but on the enormous granite boulders – either naturally occurring as at the Pierres Jaumâtres in the hills east of Pradelette, or dolmens and menhirs erected by man.

The stories surrounding the astounding Pierres Jaumâtres are fascinating. According to these tales, long long ago this hillside was the source of many hot springs. These springs had magical healing qualities appreciated by the peasant folk. But when these folk converted to Christian beliefs, they abandoned the sacred springs.

This neglect of the old customs enraged the powerful Queen of Sorcerers. Wild with fury, she leapt onto the highest stone, kicking the rock beneath her feet with venom. The healing hot springs immediately ceased to flow. Next, the witch violently hurled a heavy hammer into the skies above her, screaming "Wherever on the earth this hammer falls, there the healing springs will gush forth again".

The enchanted hammer fell to earth miles to the southeast, at Evaux-les-Bains, a town whose hot mineral-enriched natural springs have been famous for centuries for their healing qualities. Today people flock to the thermal baths in the hope of alleviating rheumatism and disorders of the circulation.

Another legend of the "Pierres" declares that the treasure of the ancient town of Toulx lies buried somewhere on this strange hillside. A golden calf leaves his lair at certain significant moments in time, blowing fire from his nostrils. "Bad luck to any guilty person who encounters him! But if a truly pure, good person chances to see the golden calf during Christmas night, during the hour of Midnight Mass, she will be able to calm the animal, who will lead her directly to the secret den in which the treasure is concealed. This fortunate person should then share the gold and riches with all the neighbourhood. This generous act will herald a golden epoch, a new era of good fortune".

I like to stand among these hulking tons of lichen-embossed rock, reminiscent of sleeping dinosaurs, remembering those long ago wily peasants who wandered this same "Jaumâtres" hillside, feeling the sun on their faces and letting their imaginations run riot.

Many are the tales of curses and spells, of wrongs committed and the righteous poor rewarded. I found these (written in French) in brochures freely available at local Tourist Offices. I have only, so far, visited a few of the sites mentioned.

On our next visit, I hope at least to investigate la Pierre d'Ep Nell, in the wooded hillsides south of Toulx Ste Croix. Young people passing this stone could ensure the good favour of benign spirits by leaving offerings in a crevice of the rock. By crawling under this same rock, a person could be freed from all digestive disorders. This I must try!

Scattered throughout this leafy countryside are myriad fascinating ruins to be discovered, such as the first century temple remains at Puy Lautard. Most of these sites of pagan or celtic origin – temples, dolmens, menhirs and so on – are now linked with the names of Christian saints: St. Pierre Bellevue and St. Priest la Feuille are examples. Many of the stones bear names hinting at the associated legends, such as "la Pierre Folle". As at Toulx, the archeological interest goes back beyond the romano-gallic times when the church and bell-tower were built, to prehistory and the mysterious burial sites and sacred places. Local museums display tools, weapons, household artefacts and jewellery from many epochs.

To return to the topic of "les Trois Lacs", created as part of the hydro-electric network stretching throughout central France. I counted fourteen barrages on my map of the Creuse Department. These lakes and rivers may look natural, but they are now controlled by man! We had startling evidence of this one burningly hot day when we decided on a trip to the lakes. We drove alongside some of the southern stretches and could see the water glinting through the trees. We heard the shouts of bathers; but on this particular afternoon, we had determined to go further north to a spot where we had enjoyed peace and tranquillity on an earlier visit. This way and that we turned, through a labyrinth of steep lanes, full of pleasurable anticipation as we passed signs with tempting pictures of divers to encourage us.

We were nearly there, the tourist signs were clear! Then, finally rolling onto a rough-mown stretch of grass at the bottom of the gorge, we gasped with astonishment. Where was the water? A vast expanse of sand, giving way to pitted mud of the river bed, stretched before us. We descended, and wandered disbelieving across what could have been a desert scene. Not a drop of water anywhere, and the sun blazing down. We were not entirely alone – another family with several children had made the descent, and stood around looking equally disconsolate and mystified. It seems that the network of lakes and rivers is under push-button control. If water is needed elsewhere, the barrage upstream is closed tight, while downstream the floodgates are opened! Goodbye water!

Sometimes, on our journey homewards after these trips to "Pays des Trois Lacs", we would drive above the higgledy-piggledy streets of Châtelus-Malvaleix. This quaint little town is only five miles from Pradelette, and is the town to which our *Taxes Foncières* and *Taxe d'Habitation* are paid. We frequently visit the good *quincaillerie*, where practically any hardware can be found and the staff take endless trouble to help us. Well, from some high roads, we could look down into a dip in the landscape where a large lake glinted in the sunshine. Tiny patches of colour could be seen – bathers, and sunbathers stretched out on grassy banks. We wondered, how do you get there? Is it a private lake attached to a private camp-site? It was far less extensive, far less dramatic, than the lake areas of La Grande Creuse – but it was so much nearer!

Eventually, of course, we found our way from the centre of the little town, down a narrow precipitous lane to this lake. Parking, access, everything we wanted, was totally free. Some parts of the reed-fringed lake are restricted to fishing, but a footpath leads through the woods, right around the lake. Once again, on first acquaintance, this lake looked entirely natural, although one area was set aside for campers. Over the years, it has sprouted several holiday *gîtes* and a tennis court, a supervised bathing area complete with lifeguard, a snack bar, slides and swings for the children, and showers for emerging bathers (totally free). Our grandchildren love it. You may still wander away from the crowded areas and watch butterflies, or the stunning turquoise or ruby-red dragonflies which dart among the rushes and purple loosestrife. So we are well satisfied.

Sometimes still, we are more adventurous. We have been as far north as Fresselines. Here, the confluence of La Petite Creuse and La Grande Creuse makes a wonderful bathing spot. Beyond this is Crozant, with medieval fortress remains on rocky promontories where the Sédelle joins the Creuse. This whole area was beloved by Monet. The "Rocher de Roche-blond" and "Pont de Vervy" are known as the *site Claude Monet*. Once again, at Crozant, the Devil is given credit for building the Pont Charraud! This bridge dates from 1603. Is the poor chap still vainly seeking a wife?

Nearer home, we have seen bathers on the banks of La Petite Creuse in the beautiful grounds of Moulin de Freteix. I suspect that when I find time to walk the footpaths which wind along-side the river at Boussac, there may be yet more places to dis-port ourselves. Deep gorges surround Boussac on two sides, and the water wriggles and snakes along the bottom. We have tackled the steep path which goes down under the *château* wall, on the south of the town, passing by enchanting little cottages right at the foot of the towering cliff. This path leads round the west of the *château*, and up into the back streets of the town. No doubt other tracks can be found to take us beyond the town, when we have time!

We must also make time one day to visit the "Plan d'eau de Courtille" near Guéret, which offers sailing and wind-surfing among its other attractions.

We actually have a beautiful rushing stream to the east of us, twenty minutes' walk away. This is the Verraux, which tumbles noisily around small islets and over its rocky uneven bed. We have never seen anyone bathing or paddling there and access seems to be over pastureland.

When we want a change from lakes and rivers, we can make forest forays in the extensive chain of hills south of Guéret. This is the Massif Forestier de Chabrières, covering the Monts de la Marche. "La Marche" is the medieval name of the district

La Chasse en Creuse

now known as the Department of the Creuse. Although I know there are dozens of specified tracks and walks in these woods and hills, and official cycling and horse-riding routes, I am a little wary of forest walking since casually picking up a leaflet about the national organisation for men hunting game of all kinds. *La chasse* is a very favoured local pursuit, and I have met ominous armed desperadoes on my walks – accompanied by dogs, sacks for the prey, and packets of sandwiches! They have always been very polite and helpful when I ask directions.

However, studying this leaflet entitled *"La Chasse en Creuse"*, I learned some uncomfortable facts. There were 224 accidents in the year 1997-8. Forty-five of these were fatalities! Another 104 people were seriously wounded. I couldn't resist a wry smile as I read that forty of these injuries were self-inflicted. No more reassuring was the knowledge that half these accidents were perpetrated by chasseurs aged fifty or over. But worse was to come: two of the dead and nineteen of the injured were not even wielding guns. One was killed by wild boar, a second while pursuing lesser game. Nine of the injured were totally unconnected with the hunt. They were not naughty trespassers who had infiltrated the fenced areas where notices declare *"Réserve au Chasse"*. Four were innocent walkers, one a cyclist, another a forest worker. Two poor souls were in their own garden at the time of injury! The account does say these unfortunate passers-by were "masked by vegetation", but that's a feeble excuse!

I always thought these *chasseurs* looked reckless and savage; whereas Suffolk chaps on a "shoot" resemble a decrepit version of "Dad's Army", these French *chasseurs* look like ruthless revolutionaries! I resolved not to be enticed into the green leafy woods unless with a large organised group of ramblers.

It is slight comfort to know these alarming statistics are for the whole of France, not just the Creuse! Interestingly, this *"Chasse"* document listed details of poaching crimes – the illicit shooting or trapping of game done secretly, out of official season, the proceeds not shared between the entire local *chasse* and also exceeding quota restrictions. Penalties included fines, periods of community service, prison sentences, withdrawal of gun licences – in short, the perpetrators are cast into outer darkness. In contrast, there is no mention at all of retribution against those who inadvertently shoot their friends and neighbours!

Bon courage indeed! We will continue sandwiching our restoration endeavours with safe leisure activities in this delectable locality.

It is lovely to know that the woods, valleys and hills of the Creuse are home to an increasing horde of wildlife living as in the garden of Eden (thanks to Government policies of conservation and protection) – until disturbed by *la chasse*. I have to admit that my own attitudes to the hunt and the hunted are ambivalent to say the least, possibly downright hypocritical. I am not vegetarian. At home, surplus cockerels go in the pot and we

An innocent denizen of the forest

85

have friends who will suddenly appear with a bag of feet and feathers which turns out to be part of the result of a pigeon-shooting outing. Then we make delectable game casserole with root vegetables, bacon and pigeon breast. But I always let others do the dirty work. My principle is that if creatures have lived a well-fed unrestricted life and their end is quick and humane, we are living as befits our bodily needs and design. After all, we do possess canine teeth! However, when I observe cloth-wrapped packages being delivered to homes in Pradelette in the days following *la chasse* and cannot help realising the silhouette of the bundle shows it to be the fore-legs of a deer, a shudder of revulsion goes down my spine.

Once again, this is illogical and hypocritical since we have friends in Germany, vineyard owners in the Mosel valley, who have fed us on wild boar and venison. And it was delicious.

"Ah, what fools these humans be," as the Bard declared!

12

NEIGHBOURS

"BON appetit!" called a small voice as we sat down to supper *au plein air.* Six-year-old Alexander beamed at us from the garden next door. He took particular interest in our arrangements on this evening since we were seated around a huge insulated plastic board, balanced precariously on our smaller table. This object, obtained by Alexander's uncle who works in the freezer department of a supermarket, had been dragged around and triumphantly offered to us as a gift by Alexander's grandmother Nicole, who obviously felt our little table was far too small for a decent-sized meal! This typifies the generosity of our neighbours.

We were a great novelty in this French hamlet. There are only seven inhabited houses in the place. Two average-sized farmhouses are currently used to accommodate chickens, hay and grain. Two minute houses stand empty, although one of these possesses a barn let to a local farmer for his sheep. One of these little houses, in prime position on the south-facing slopes of the long valley, was until recently the home of an elderly lady who kept goats and made cheese. Sadly there are now no goats in this village.

The three smartest houses are all owned by elderly French couples who moved from towns in the area to enjoy a country retirement. We have never got to know any of these well. They probably think we are very odd. Another farmhouse stands totally unmodernised, in a largish grassy garden with a stone well as its central feature, complete with wind-up handle. Here live Daniel and his mother (well into her eighties). Daniel was a farm worker and now devotes his time to his mother, his cat and his drinking friends.

Our *fermette* has farms on three sides and pastureland on the fourth (west) side. We have made lasting friendships with these nearest neighbours who have been kindness itself. They have invited us into their homes, and showered us with gifts during the first six or seven years (the gifts seemed to slacken off as the years rolled on but the friendly overtures remain!). At first, we were liable to receive huge bags of vegetables from all three directions, resulting in frequent gluts, particularly of *haricots verts*, which became rather a joke. The path through our back garden and down Ron's new steps became known as "the *haricot vert* path". We received gifts of every seasonal fruit and vegetable, plus flowers, eggs, chestnuts, walnuts, and wild mushrooms. We have even been given floor *pamments* and bricks, an old milk churn, and a specially made frilly cushion!

One never-to-be-forgotten gift came in a large washing-up bowl. There lay around eighty small clumsy-looking river fish, recommended as delicious. Madame explained that they should be dusted with flour, then fried.

Well, I abandoned my stair-building and spent the rest of the afternoon trying to gut and clean these muddy little creatures. They had strange swim-bladders and ugly faces.

We had eight in residence at our *fermette* that day – some friends, some family – and during the afternoon two more friends arrived. I thought, well at least we have plenty of fish! I cooked them in batches, getting the fat as hot as possible. I hoped they would be rather like sprats, which I love.

We laid our long table outside, under the buddleias, in

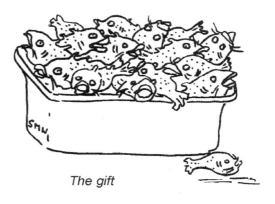

The gift

happy anticipation, and in went the forks... oh dear! The fish tasted unpleasantly muddy; but the real problem was the bones. Terrible spiky bones radiated out from the backbone, and other small insidious bones seemed to lurk in every corner of the flesh. Our well brought-up friends and family persisted in the struggle, trying hard to look as though they were enjoying a fabulous delicacy, but it was no good. One by one we all gave up, and the fish ended up in the hedge-bottom. I prayed they would not poison or choke anybody's chickens or cats!

Next day Madame smilingly enquired whether we had enjoyed the fish. I tried to look her in the eye and say how interesting we had found them – but something about my voice or demeanour must have told her the truth. A few hours later she appeared bearing a beautiful *Creusoise* cake which she had baked for us. The ingredients included butter, eggs, and ground hazelnuts. It was a delight and this time our thanks were genuine!

When I first decided to build stairs, our Swiss neighbours (owners of the Friesian herd) said we could take as much stone as we wanted from a tumble-down outhouse and garden wall at the back of their barns. We staggered about with sagging knees, bringing home the best, flattest stones. From time to time Paul would arrive on our land with his fork-lift, on which would be heaped particularly large flat stones which he thought would make good steps. We never had to worry about having sufficient stone until, in our seventh year of ownership, this family suddenly upped sticks and moved back to Switzerland. The financial worries of farm ownership became too much for them and they went as tenants to care for a Holstein herd near Lac de Joux.

Their farm was bought by Olivier and Liliane, who keep sheep. Many years ago Liliane worked as an au-pair in London. She is the only villager to speak any English.

One October, Ron and I were joined by friends Anne and Alan and we decided to collect wood for a fire. We had been told by neighbours that the woods north of the village are

The bread van calls!

owned by a man in Paris who never comes anywhere near, so it is possible to collect wood there. We found plenty lying around, although it was distinctly damp. We staggered home and lit our fire and settled down for a cosy evening. Then the door burst open. There stood Andrée and Guy, lugging enormous hunks of tree-root nearly as big as themselves! Of course they were invited in and the fire burned brighter warming all our hearts.

Over the years, we have made friends in other villages. News of our presence spread. One dear old man, Georges, very much wanted to meet us as his only daughter teaches English at the local secondary school. He cycled up and down the street in his village when we were walking there, finally plucking up courage to talk to us. Georges is a smallholder and bee-keeper. During the war, aged seventeen, he was transported to Hungary by the Germans to work in a factory there. He escaped, managed to get home and spent the rest of the war using the identity documents of his deceased grandfather and ready to hide in the roof-space if ever a house-search were to occur. He and his wife Odette make us excessively welcome and we have sampled many a dusty ancient bottle of their own distilled fruit liqueurs.

Other elderly folk from villages round about now treat us as friends even though we may chat to them rarely – once a year maybe. People are in short supply in these districts and anyone new is an event. I remember our first chat with a lady living a mile away, across the River Verraux. Throughout our conversation Juliet and I could not keep our eyes away from her hands. They were immensely broad and strong, like the digging hands of a mole. She was shorter than either of us, but with strength in her shoulders and arms – we could see why, as she had heavy buckets of water in each hand, and every time I have spoken to her since, she has been hard at work in barn or garden. This hard life has left her with the sweetest, most courteous and contented expression and manner. We feel humble in her presence.

One or two confrontations have been so unusual as to merit chapters of their own. Read on!

13

JACQUES THE LAD

"IT'S a beautiful night – let's go for a walk."

"OK. But where shall we go?"

"I'd rather not walk along the main road – let's drive to one of the villages, park the van and see what's going on."

"Right – who's coming, then?"

So it was that one fine August evening three of us set out: myself, Linda, my friend and colleague, and Juliet, my youngest daughter. Ron, and Juliet's partner Eddie, opted to stay at Pradelette and get on with building the terrasse.

We drove a couple of miles and parked on a wide verge. Opposite our stopping place was a field of sprightly brown goats and assorted poultry, alongside a farmhouse with lighted windows. Dogs barked, and a stocky rosy faced man in overalls appeared. He was barely five feet in height, but immensely broad shoulders gave an impression of great strength. He regarded us with close interest, enquiring whether we had stopped because of a breakdown.

We managed to assure him that our van was not *"en panne"* – we simply wanted to walk. He seemed puzzled and disappointed by this, having obviously hoped to rescue three damsels in distress. On hearing we were intent on walking to the next village, he pleaded with us to come into his house and "have a little drink" with him first. There was such appeal in his face and voice that we agreed (safety in numbers!).

So it was that we entered Jacques' kitchen, an odorous and crowded area, every inch of table, cupboard top, fridge, and even some parts of the floor, being covered by elegant earthenware jars in which soft goats' cheese was in various stages of

Chez Jacques

maturation. Two large black-and-white collies eventually over-came their excitement at the visitation, and settled down on our feet, under the table. Enough space was created for tiny glasses to be given round, and we were plied with spirit home-made by Jacques himself from pure distilled pear juice – very mature, very *"forte"*, and only given to very special guests. He showed us how to make the potent liqueur more palatable by adding sugar cubes. Then, beaming with rapture, he proceed-ed to chat us up (all three at once!).

He told Linda (recently widowed) that she was *très très belle* and would certainly quickly find a new husband. He expressed desolation on hearing that Juliet (aged twenty-four) had a partner back at the *fermette* so was spoken for. He glowed, his face becoming ever more florid as he threw himself into entertaining three friendly ladies. When I asked after his wife (I had seen her in the garden on previous occasions) he said she was busy with the goats and chickens and would soon come indoors.

Darkness fell outside. We finished the pear and started on some peach liqueur. Jacques grew effusive, we grew giggly and foolish. Finally to his regret, we thanked him and rose to leave (his wife never materialised) and Jacques escorted us outside, enormous arms enfolding at least two of us "beautiful ladies" at a time; he seemed to have more than the usual quota of hands which were everywhere at once (maybe his caresses would have been less embarrassing if he had been taller, said Linda!).

We invited him to visit us one day, and meet the rest of our party. Wistfully, he watched us leave, glowing with fervour, perspiration and bonhomie in the dusk.

We decided we were none of us in a fit state to drive. We walked uncertainly, still laughing excessively, into the next village, where we chatted with various residents at the open doors of their houses. Goodness knows what we said to them! When we began to feel a little steadier, we groped our way back in the darkness to where the van waited, very quietly so as not to disturb Jacques. We got safely home by a novel and unexpected route, not much the worse for wear.

Some days later, talking to our friend Dominique, a neighbour of Jacques and teacher of English at the local secondary school, we learned that dear Jacques was well known for his great weakness for women. Dominique told us of a time when the village was flooded, and a pharmacist friend of hers, needing to get to work, was "helped" by Jacques who insisted on carrying her through several stretches of deep water. As Dominique said: "She 'ad a leetle trouble weez 'eem – but it was not serious!"

We agreed – it was not serious. It was good to see a chap so blissfully happy. And we were all sorry to learn, about a year later, that Jacques had died suddenly from a heart attack at the age of fifty-nine.

We felt privileged to have shared one convivial evening with Jacques among the goat cheeses.

14

THE DEMON DRINK

"VOULEZ-vous quelque chose à boire?"
"Non, merci... oh, merci... seulement un peu, s'il vous plait..."
"Voila!"
"Sante!"
"A la votre!"
"...encore un peu, peut-être?"
"Non, merci... oh, merci... c'est vraiment assez..."
"Santé!"... and so on. The drinks are poured, generously as usual. Tentatively we sip our pastis and add a little more water. Also as usual, we have been given far more alcohol than our hosts are drinking. It is bad form for any host to neglect to do this, and it happens even in homes where the wife of the host refuses to drink anything except fruit juice or water. She is allowed to decline, we the guests are not. So we smile all round, and drink slowly. If we empty our glasses, more will immediately be poured in.

Most of our neighbours are moderate in their drinking. But for anyone with a weakness for alcohol France must be a dangerous place – it is freely offered around, in every home, at virtually any time of day or night, at the least possible excuse. Go to a tradesman, for instance, to arrange some business, and the bargain will be sealed with drinks all round. Wine flows during meals and on every social occasion. We keep intending to take more glasses to our *fermette* to be prepared for the arrival of casual guests. We normally buy the big plastic containers of basic red or rosé to drink with the evening meal. We tend to be sparing with wine at lunch time, or we would never get any work done. On one memorable heat-wave of a day, Linda, Ron and I each had a small glassful with our frugal lunch. The heat was blistering so we repaired to our respective beds for "a little siesta" before starting work again. Not one of us woke until after 5pm! We were shocked... we had missed a whole afternoon's work. Where did we think we were, on holiday or something?

In my childhood family, any suggestion of alcoholic refreshment was anathema. My mother had been brought up a Methodist, my father a Baptist. At church, we were encouraged to join the "GAYS"...yes, honestly! This was the 1950s, remember! "GAYS" were the "Guild of Abstaining Youth"! Sounds attractive? After the hoots of ribald laughter, it would go down like a lead balloon today, and was not too popular then. However, we obediently joined and signed the pledge (I was about thirteen at the time). The GAYS ran so-called "social evenings" in dim church halls in the town. A few unsavoury looking youths would be present, and some giggly girls. There might be a short talk on the evils of drink, some sandwiches and tea, and a few games or dances (Gay Gordons?) just to convince us we were having fun. I didn't want to go anywhere near these tongue-tied lads, let alone dance with them. They seemed to have spotty greenish complexions and feel as awkward as they looked. But at the age of fifteen I did go on a GAY holiday in the Peak District, where I met my first serious boyfriend (he was serious, not me). He was twenty and owned a car which was very exciting. He was a Quaker from a farming family. I just wanted someone to go around with, but we corresponded for several years. He visited our home, which I found alarming. Then I extricated myself. Somehow, my sister and I also extricated ourselves from the "GAY community"...or perhaps it just fizzled out because it was so truly boring.

Ironically, this church which fostered the GAY club also ran a line in "ginger beer plants". These were smelly concoctions of sugar, active yeast, ginger and a little water, which had to be kept in luke-warm conditions, the liquid being drawn off at intervals and drunk. It was frothy and sickly-sweet. There was a kind of mystique about these "plants" – if a friend gave you one, you were honour-bound to nurture it and keep it "alive" (a little like a modern day cyber pet, maybe!).

Another odd aspect was that I had never even seen anyone drinking to excess. There were no pubs in our neighbourhood, and I never even went into a pub until after I was eighteen and at training college, when a group of us walked over the moors to a Yorkshire village pub. (After my mother's eightieth birthday party we, her children and grandchildren, took her to a country pub. It was the first time she had entered such a place and she seemed mildly surprised to see how innocuous it was.)

It was true that some branches of our family might imbibe a scandalous glass of sherry on such occasions as a christening or wedding. This vice was on a par with certain other shocking habits, such as the wearing of lipstick. When I did get a chance to sample the forbidden nectar, I was singularly unimpressed. I have never liked the smell of beer. But cider, shandy, anything with refreshing lime or lemon juice in it, wine, liqueurs, port, sherry, and small amounts of sweetish spirit are OK by me. I don't seem to have gone down the path to destruction yet, and really I'd just as soon have orange juice (sacrilege!).

As demonstrated by Jacques and George, in the Creuse it was traditional for country folk to distil fruit juice for their own use. Professional distillers did the rounds of the villages in autumn, or some families had a kind of hereditary licence to do their own distilling. This has now become an illegal activity, but I'm sure it still continues. Every family seems to have a few "special bottles" tucked away in dark cupboards and cellars, which they delight in sharing.

Our friend Alan is something of a wine buff. He gave us the four beautiful vines which flourish on the south wall of our *fermette* – two white, and two black grapes. The whites are Muscat of Alexandria, a very prolific cropper, described as "a classical golden grape". Then we have Chasselas Rosé, an ancient variety originating in Germany and also much favoured in Switzerland. This bears large variously coloured grapes. Our black varieties are Gagarin Blue (from Russia of course!) and Valentina Tereschkova, also from Russia. These two varieties are said to have been acquired by a vine devotee in exchange for a box of biros!

Our vines have the most gorgeously tinted autumn leaves. They look enchanting with the gnarled twisting stem and branches well ensconced among the rugged stonework, and with a profusion of green, yellow and gold leaves surrounding doors and windows. We have to be a bit careful when shutting doors; we are liable to crush several bunches of delectable grapes between door and frame. (Old joke: What did the grape say when the elephant trod on it? Answer – nothing. It just gave a little wine!)

There is also a vine bearing sweet black grapes entwined in our roadside hedge. We thought this was wild, but neighbour Andrée assures us that long ago it was deliberately planted there and carefully tended. We have had magnificent harvests from all these vines, which are all excellent dessert grapes as well as good for wine-making. Alan generously produces superb wine from our grape harvest. On his Suffolk small-holding he also has an apple-crushing machine, home-made from bits of machinery, and makes cider from our Creusoise apples. We try to take samples of each vintage back to France to give our neighbours – to show we can join them at their own game, I suppose. It is much appreciated.

Another friend, Graham, will produce elderberry wine if we pick the berries. You may ask why we don't make our own wine. I think we are not careful enough, not patient and exact and in my case, just not scientific in my thinking. I have tried. I picked cowslips and primroses and made quantities of wine vinegar. This I tucked away for several years, in the hope that it would miraculously become "vintage". But no... as soon as I could bring myself to discard it, I did so. My elderberry exploded unaided. We also had a recipe for a kind of marrow rum. We had to hang up a large marrow in a plastic bag, first making an incision and pouring in ginger and sugar, leaving it in a dark cupboard to "mature". The result was predictable, and that cupboard has never been quite the same since. But we are very good at sloe gin. We don't confine ourselves to sloes, having used damsons and bullaces as well. And we don't confine ourselves to gin – brandy or even whisky will do. Soaked for a few months in the spirit, with plenty of added brown sugar, this becomes a delicious brew, great to drink around a winter fireside.

On the whole, the French affinity with wine and alcohol of all kinds complements their general character – laid back, generous, hospitable, and always ready to enjoy the good things of life. It oils the wheels of friendship. Also, as shown by our friend with the rakish panama and unsteady step who was such a dab hand at stripping roofs, alcohol renders the French even more ready to help their fellow men!

15

"UNE PETITE SOTTISE"

"LOOK at that! Ron said there was a big difference between two-star and the others! But I never thought it would be that much cheaper!"

"Good, you might as well fill up, then, while we're here."

"Might as well – and then, we must remember to look for a bin and dump the *ordures*."

There are no dustbins in Pradelette, so we tie our rubbish in plastic bags and take it for a ride to the nearest collection point. Today we had five obnoxious bags to dispose of. The trip to Boussac was mainly to buy supplies at the supermarket. We'd acquired a cooked marinated chicken and some weird-looking vegetables – celeriac, *navet long* and aubergines – just for a change; and of course, cheeses, fruit and plenty of wine.

Having filled up the van we set off for home with the glow of satisfied bargain hunters. As we swept out of the town on the switchback bends near the clifftop *château*, I realised the contents of the rubbish bags were still making their presence felt. Never mind, there were bins at the side of the road further on.

But what was that grating sound? Something was seriously wrong with the van. The engine struggled, groaned, gasped and died! Even as we stopped, a dreadful realisation flooded into my mind. No wonder filling up had been cheap – I had filled the van with DIESEL instead of petrol! I've always had a bit of a blockage with these terms – *"gazole"* somehow reminded me of the American "gas". But of course, petrol was *"essence"*. How could I have forgotten that? What an idiot.

We were now alarmingly placed on a steep bend. I had horrible forebodings, that we would cause an accident to cars coming simultaneously around the corners to find us sticking well out into the road. I ran farther up the hill and flapped at on-coming traffic like a demented windmill. Luckily there was very little traffic, but I got some funny looks. About five minutes later,

Corner of La Terrade near Jalesches

a car stopped and three concerned-looking people got out. My French was strained to the utmost as I struggled to explain – no, we had not run out of petrol; we had accidentally filled up with diesel.

Our rescuers were kindness itself. The son, Eric, stayed with us while his parents drove into Boussac to seek help. In no time, it seemed, a break-down van arrived and our crippled vehicle was towed to a garage for a cleaning-up operation that would take three days.

Now our new friends insisted on taking us home. We felt more than a little socially unacceptable. Not only did we have bags of groceries with us – we had five stinking bags of *ordures*! Red-faced, we climbed gratefully into the back seat of their spotless vehicle with our sordid collection.

I will draw a veil over the reception we received on arriving at the *fermette* where Ron was working away single-handed. Luckily for me, his response to my feeble attempts at explanation was a little toned down by the presence of three fascinated French good Samaritans. The best move seemed to be, to offer cups of calming English tea all round. The frenzied excuses and indignant recriminations died away... for after all, what's done is done.

In fact, this small family became our good friends and remain so. Eric spent the next August with us in England, hoping to improve his English. His parents have been endlessly helpful, in such dilemmas as how to make an insurance claim, and where to buy terracotta tiles. They also gave us a glory-vine which flourishes on our front wall, helping to camouflage the cracks.

So we made new friends; and another bit of expensive learning was achieved. This was a ridiculous mistake. I promise, it will happen only once!

16

"MUSIC WHILE YOU WORK"

"STOP working, Sheila. Come here and sit down. I want to sing something to you."

I did as I was told. Patricia was grinning wickedly. Then she began to sing, the plaintive tune being a Hungarian folk-song which we had spent our evenings learning. But the song usually began "By a river, there's a little orchard..."

"In the stable there's a little bucket,
In the bucket just a little water,
In the bucket just a little water.

Sheila, Sheila, don't you think you oughta
Get some sand to make a little mortar,
Get some sand to make a little mortar.

So she went to town and there she bought a
Bag or two of sand to make some mortar,
Bag or two of sand to make some mortar.

Then she mixed it just as Ron had taught her,
Sand, cement and lime, and then some water,
Sand, cement and lime, and then some water.

Sheila, Sheila, can we help you sort a
Stone or two, to place upon your mortar,
Stone or two, to place upon your mortar.

No, she said, I had a little thought a

'Bout the stones, the bucket and the mortar,
What I really need is just a porter.

Walls grow higher, days are getting shorter,
In the bucket, just a little mortar,
In the bucket, just a little mortar."

By the time she finished, our eyes were streaming with tears of laughter. We wanted to hear it again... and again! I felt proud – no one has ever written a song about me before. I tried to emulate her, writing little ditties to fit the other songs of the cycle; but nothing matched this first comical effort. One lovely result of owning the *fermette* is, that we have spent time with various friends whom we normally rarely see.

We have known Patricia and Michael for over forty years but for most of this time we have lived hundreds of miles apart. Like us, they have seven children. Unlike us, they had the fore-thought to name their children A-B-C-D-E-F-G. We waited, wondering whether Horace or Hermione would arrive next – but no, Adrian was first, Gemma last.

We did a lot of singing during their Creuse visit. The highlight came when we entered the tiny romano-gallic church at Toulx-Ste-Croix. Looking up into the gaily painted dome shaped sanctuary, spontaneously we sang *"Dona Nobis Pacem"*

The Bell Tower, Toulx-Ste-Croix

104

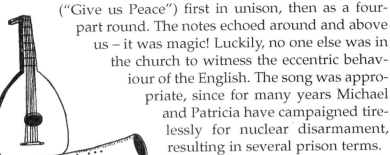

("Give us Peace") first in unison, then as a four-part round. The notes echoed around and above us – it was magic! Luckily, no one else was in the church to witness the eccentric behaviour of the English. The song was appropriate, since for many years Michael and Patricia have campaigned tirelessly for nuclear disarmament, resulting in several prison terms.

We often take instruments with us, hoping the thick walls will keep the dubious sounds from

Medieval lute and cornett

our neighbours' ears. Ron takes brass and guitar, I my violin. Our Swiss neighbours (now returned to Switzerland) love music, and Pauline plays the accordion with skill and sensitivity; so sometimes we enjoyed shared sessions. We tried to learn Swiss folk-songs.

Most summers there are concerts in local churches when quaint old tunes are played on lutes and hurdy-gurdies. Audiences tend to be unlike typical English audiences at such events. Whole families attend, including their menfolk, many still wearing bright blue farming overalls. There is no elitism about the event – everyone goes, and enjoys it.

Sometimes we have happened upon marvellous village entertainments which are totally free. In the village of Soumans we spent hours listening to Edwardian music-hall and drawing-room songs, interspersed with clog dances and old songs from the Creuse. Even the refreshments were free (but not the drinks!). Another time, we made slow progress up the hills of the Pierres Jaumâtres, pausing among the mossy rocks to hear excerpts from the legends of Arthur and Guinevere, accompanied by dances, hurdy-gurdy, bagpipes, lutes and singing (and we believed Arthur and Guinevere's colourful lives were spent in south-west England! How wrong we were!)

The Creuse is full of surprises.

17

"WE ARE NOT ALONE"

"WAKE up... Ron, wake up, please..."

I finally got my husband to at least half open his eyes.

"Whatever is it, what's the matter?"

"I had a dream about the sea, the waves were splashing all around, I think I was in some kind of boat, and then I woke up, and the splashing's coming from under our bed...listen!"

Reluctantly he listened, and there it was again. Now our bed on this chilly October visit was in the living room alongside the fire-place. We banked up the fire each evening and could see the embers glowing through the night, ready to be poked into new life the next morning (just as in long ago days in rustic France). But there were no water pipes anywhere in this room, so what was it? I fumbled for my torch, and looked in trepidation under the bed.

"Oh no! This is awful! There's a poor little mouse swimming round and round in the chamber pot!"

What to do? I was paralysed by shock and indecision. Ron refused to accept the seriousness of the situation and was struggling against sleep. I thought, how can I fish the mouse out without putting my hand in? Suppose I tip the lot into the garden, surely the little shivering thing will freeze to death? Meanwhile, the poor little creature drowned. What a terrible way to die!

Our *fermette* has always been a dwelling place. But during the fifty years before I bought it, it was a dwelling place for animals, not people. Villagers remember it being used as a stable until thirty years ago. But even when the horses were gone, it continued to be home to many creatures.

The walls are at least sixty centimetres thick, more in some parts. The middle section is a mixture of loose rubble plus the nest remnants of many creatures. If Ron needs to make a hole for a waste pipe, within the outer "built" areas of wall he delves into this loose centre, made even looser than

Quel horreur!

it was originally by the passage of beetles, spiders, lizards by the hundred, hibernating butterflies and moths, mice (and worse!), who have scurried about their business over centuries. Bats emerge from the rafters at dusk and swoop around the garden. Small birds nest in nooks and crannies between the stones. Quite large birds seem to have taken up residence from time to time in the larger holes within the house walls. I once found a chicken's egg in a deep hole twelve feet above the floor! And there were silvery owl pellets on the *grenier* floor.

Scores of swallows adorn the telegraph wires in the summer. All the village barns, and our own stable, had mud nests firmly fixed to their beams. On our arrival one August I decided to brush down one of these ancient-looking nests, since crumbs of mud were apt to fall into our plates during meals. I used a long-handled brush to dislodge it. To my absolute horror, as it fell to the floor I realised it wasn't empty. Four little heads poked upwards in distress. They were fledgling sparrows, almost ready to leave the nest. The terrified parents flew round our heads in a panic. I felt like a murderer; but by a miracle the young ones were not harmed. We hastily tied the remaining nest material, complete with fledglings, to the top of a beam, and were able to spend the next few days watching as the mother persuaded her brood to make the first fluttering attempts and launch themselves into space. All four success-fully flew away.

These tiny sparrows, smaller and more sleek than our English ones and with pink undersides to their little bodies, constantly fly in and out of cracks in all the village buildings and seem ready to set up home in any nook or cranny.

Of course we have mice of many varieties – black, brown, shaggy or smooth coated, large and small. They are sometimes endearingly tame, not having learned that man is their enemy, but we can't allow them the freedom of the house since we have cushions, stored bedding and shelves of china which we prefer not to be decorated with their leavings. Our neighbour Nicole lets her cats into our house regularly when we are away, to help keep numbers in check. But the *fermette* is their home and no doubt will continue to be so. Maybe we, not they, are the intruders.

So-called domestic animals in this village live an unusually free and independent life. Gardens are mostly open; the barri-ers tend to be around vegetable plots to keep out the maraud-ing poultry. This arrangement, rather the opposite of English habits when it is the poultry who are wired in, not the vegeta-bles, was confusing at first. During the second visit to view the house before buying, it's surprising the three of us didn't alien-ate the neighbours entirely since we walked right through a private farmyard thinking it was a public track (no fences) and wandered around our neighbour Andrée's lawn assuming it to be a kind of village green.

The ducks, geese and chickens of Pradelette live a kind of communal life during the day and only go to their separate quarters at night to be fed and housed by their respective own-ers. So we may be interrupted at breakfast by a trail of ducks investigating our open doorway, or find hens under our table searching for crumbs. I love this atmosphere, and was inspired to keep ducks and hens again in Suffolk (after keeping only geese for several years). Now in England as in France, we wake in the mornings to their comforting chatter. Luckily Ron and I

Some of our neighbours

both find crowing cockerels enjoyable rather than disturbing, probably because both of us in early childhood were used to poultry in garden shacks, providing a welcome boost to our family rations during and after the war.

During our earlier visits, we were entertained by a large and belligerent black turkeycock who daily patrolled the pasture adjoining our garden. He obviously believed he was boss of the outfit – probably, boss of the whole of creation as he perceived it to be. He was outraged and indignant at our uninvited presence in his kingdom. He would puff himself up and fluff out all his feathers, quivering with rage, then emit two or three loud "honks" from deep in his throat (a little like a bullfrog) just to put us in our place. He also "gobbled" noisily from time to time. He had extraordinary bright red and blue wattles and other dangly bits around his head and neck. For this reason we nicknamed him "Monsieur giblets-on-the-outside"! His dangly bits looked very inconvenient when he pecked for food.

They drooped and wobbled, hanging lower than his beak, so that I feared he would peck them rather than the grain he was after. Sadly, he overdid his aggression eventually; not content with bullying his several wives, he pecked a defenceless goose around the head so viciously that she had to be put in the pot before her time. This episode sealed his fate, and swiftly he got his come-uppance from farmer Paul. But I'm sure he did not die in vain!

Not all the wildlife is endearing. One year I was quite enchanted by the sweet sounds of young animals squeaking down the natural drain, built up with stones to prevent mud falling in, which is a few yards from our stable door. Then one day I saw a large rat slink down the hole. Appalled, I told our neighbour Nicole whose garden adjoins ours at this point. She was not remotely disturbed by the news. I think rats are regarded as a nuisance, but endemic – to be kept down by dogs, but never absent for long.

I should not have been surprised by the presence of rats, since during our first year of ownership I spent days sweeping out thick layers of grain-husks mixed with ancient rat-droppings from the farming end of the building.

When we planted our four vines, we were warned by neighbours that enormous hornets would come after the fruit. They were right – wasps and hornets discovered ample nesting places between the old stones, and Ron spent much of one summer visit smoking them out and in-filling the crevices. We bought an expensive bottle of fluid said to attract, then drown them. This concoction was ignored; but my home-made traps were greatly successful. These were jars half-filled with watery jam, with a small hole bored in the lid, hung in and around the vines. I believe the smell of the decomposing bodies of foolish friends and relatives was an even greater attraction than the odour of jam!

We were a little troubled by the appearance of these insects since Guy, our neighbour, is dangerously allergic to stings. But the locality abounds with plum, peach and pear trees, and vines grow unchecked in hedges. So we feel we cannot be held entirely responsible.

Seven years into ownership, I unfortunately developed an allergy myself, to the stings of mosquitoes and of even the tiniest of midges. Dreadful inflamed blisters followed their assaults on my flesh. During two successive visits, I spent days unable to wear any kind of footwear since these blisters were worst on my legs and feet. Some were over an inch across, and they did not so much itch as hurt. I didn't know where to put my poor limbs and sleep became impossible. Several times I ventured into local towns bare-footed, to the consternation of old French inhabitants who were quite open about asking me the problem. Anti-histamine tablets helped; but under these watery blisters my flesh seemed to be slowly dissolving into raw cavities. I returned home barefoot and with my poor legs exposed (I could not bear the touch of clothing on the blisters) causing other passengers on the ferry to recoil from my presence in horror. I did not need to ring a bell and shout "unclean"! At least I got a whole sofa to myself for that night crossing.

Since then, I have always gone to France armed with a good supply of anti-histamine tablets to be swallowed at the first itch! Thank goodness, this works – the scars from my sufferings took several months to heal. I enjoyed the horrified sympathy and the notoriety but it's an experience not to be repeated.

During our first summer visit, we cleared several heaps of rotting timber, both inside and outside the building. In one large crumbling log, I discovered several enormous stag beetle larvae. They were almost as long, and as fat, as my finger. We replaced them in a corner – it seemed a shame for them not to survive after over a year of solid feeding! We never saw them again.

In the evenings, toads of all sizes scramble around the mossy stones on the north side of the *fermette*. We hope they are after the horrific bright-orange slugs that stretch to incredible length on the grass. Likewise, we hope "our" sun-worshipping lizards, of all shades of brown, blue and green, are keeping down the numbers of indoor creepy-crawlies.

The local *chasse* have special days for hunting each species of animal from the dense local woods. *Reynards* or foxes are pursued, also many types of deer, and partridge, pheasants, hares, rabbits, even wild boar. There are strict limits controlling the number of days in the year on which hunting can take place, also the numbers to be culled. Even so, we never see the amount of game that Suffolk lanes reveal. Of course, French woods are larger and more remote, and maybe their game is wiser than ours.

We are not avid birdwatchers and are woefully ignorant of bird life. But in this locality even the most ignorant cannot fail to notice the abundance of hovering, swooping predators – angular kites appear against the bright blue of the sky; kestrels, hawks and even eagles thrive in these hills and woods. We try to remember to take binoculars and learn more about them.

Both countryside and buildings hide many wild creatures living their lives alongside ours. We continue to make new discoveries, while knowing that the Creuse and its wilder inhabitants will never give up all their secrets to us newcomers.

18

"FINE WORDS BUTTER NO PARSNIPS"

AS Miles Kington has remarked, the French nation do not speak O-Level French. Nor do we English go around speaking O-Level English. Languages are such complex affairs, never static, and involving shared knowledge, experience, literature and gestures, short-cuts, slang and idiom; not to mention regional differences, accents and intonation.

There is no way you can learn a few hundred words and the rudiments of grammar and end up fluent. Although my own French has improved since owning our *fermette*, I still write and read French much more easily than I speak it. I may prepare a few phrases in my head and surprise a neighbour; but when she responds at double speed I may be totally lost. I've tried to explain this disparity, saying that when I speak, I use only the words and structures I know, whereas their reply may include words I have never heard of.

Anyone who has tried speaking a foreign language will know that when you think you are pronouncing a word or a place-name perfectly the locals may look strained and baffled. Suddenly one of them will realise what you are trying to say, give a broad smile and pronounce "your" word with an impossible strangulated choking sound which you certainly were not taught in your schooldays! On other occasions, they will "correctly" pronounce a word we have struggled with, and to our English ears, their pronunciation sounds identical to ours and yet they couldn't understand what we were saying! It's a puzzle, and although I pride myself on ability to communicate at a basic level with our lovely neighbours, I sometimes catch a look of desperate forced concentration on their faces when I am in mid-flow. Also, conversations tend to dry up once we have exchanged the usual pleasantries – comments on the weather and the like – we cannot exchange any more complex thoughts, and we are left merely smiling fatuously at one another. There is *"entente cordiale"*, but not at any great depth.

We have just a few French friends who attempt English when we are with them. We are very reluctant ever to correct them. A particular difficulty is the mysterious English H, which is such a puzzle that great efforts are made to insert it wherever a word begins with a vowel. Thus we hear of a friend who works at the airport as a "hair controller". There are other problems of delivery – the French make more sounds between words than we do. When speaking English and searching for the next word, some of our French friends tend to emit a nasal groaning sound which we seldom hear on this island (except perhaps when a politician is trying to evade the issue!).

My husband seems often to be afflicted with a sudden attack of proverbs, idiom and slang when we are with French friends trying to share our thoughts. So a conversation may go like this:

Me: Come over here, Ron!

Ron: Hang on, I'm a bit tied up at the moment!

Me: Do you want any of these stones before I take them?

Ron: Wait a sec, let the dog see the rabbit – no thanks.

Me: Maybe this nice flat one? – Oops!

Ron: Butterfingers! One down, a bag of nuts!

Me: Can we get this one out?

Ron: Have you lost your marbles? It's enormous!

Me: But if I just lever this end up...

Ron: Blow that for a game of soldiers!

Me: OK. But you've nearly finished the *terrasse* – remember how Pete said you'd never do it?

Ron: Yes, and he'll soon be laughing on the other side of his face!

Me: Then we can celebrate by going out for a meal.

Ron: That's pushing the boat out a bit!

Me: Don't worry, I'll pay this time.

Ron: No skin off my nose, then!

He has even been known to try and translate these phrases word by word. It doesn't help!

When we visit tourist attractions, the brochures written by the French for their English visitors sometimes have us in

Majestic Sarzay

fits of laughter, and we feel a little less abashed by our own mistakes. Here are some of my favourites:

Leaflet describing the Maze at Guéret: "An original amusement for youngs and adults. The giant maze is not constituted of hedges. It's a paths sown-grass seed maze separated by little fences."

Description of Sarzay: "A lot of furnished rooms have kept their authenticity and at the top of the towers where there is a superb skeleton, you can see the loveliness of the landscape. Some restored deep moat, the chapel, the sked complete the beauty spot."(We searched in vain for the sked!)

Culan *château*: "...the public can visit the watcher rooms with outstanding frameworks and the hoardings made of wood, defence system of the Middle Ages, settled on the top of the towers."

My all-time favourite comes from an account of a summer *manifestation* at Chénérailles. Here is the story of Sheherazade: "Thousand and One Nights. The Sultan of Bagdad is persuaded that every woman will be unfaithful to him so he takes every night some new wife so that she will be executed before sunrise by his Vezir, Sheherazade convinces her father the Vezir, to be the new Sultan because she finds a trick to be prevented from the execution. Late at night, she undertakes to tell one of these long and marvellous tales she keeps secret. Suddenly day is rising up! Her husband who has heard with interest thinks: "let's her live until the next night because of being so much curious to know the following". So during thousand and one nights Sheherazade charms her husband and saves her life by always endind and beginning again tales."

We missed this particular *manifestation*. It sounds fascinating. Long live the phrase-book!

19

A GREAT SADNESS

THIS account of our venture into ownership of a second home in France would not be complete without mention of my dear brother David. If it were not for David, and his wife Nicole, I would never seriously have entertained such an enterprise.

I grew up in a family of four – two girls, two boys. My brother David, three years younger than I, was always a great friend to me; we enjoyed the same jokes, and most importantly, he always stood up for me, right into adulthood. But since I left home when David was still a schoolboy, to train as a teacher, then married the month I left college, moved a hundred miles south and got busy producing seven children, David and I didn't see a great deal of each other (although he was always a brilliant letter writer).

Because I was so fond of my brother, I named my first child after him. This, I realised later, was rather a foolish move, leading to a great deal of confusion. Later my sister married – another David! Once when all three "Davids" were staying in my parents' home, my brother-in-law remarked plaintively: "I always know when your mother is talking to me. Because when she says "David darling" she's addressing her son, when she says "David dear" it's her grandson, and when she just says "David" I know she means me!"

My brother David went to Oxford to read Politics, Philosophy and Economics. In Oxford he met Nicole, whose home was Guadeloupe, although she attended boarding school in France as a girl. They were married by the time David began working for his PhD. After this he launched into a very varied career, much of it abroad. They lived in Geneva,

Tanzania, Botswana, Kenya, Washington DC, Senegal and Chad. These overseas postings were interspersed with brief spells in London. Mostly he was in advisory or consultancy posts, working for the Ford Foundation, for Crown Agents, for the World Bank, and sometimes seconded to Government departments of various African countries. It was an exciting life for his sons – especially as visits to maternal grandparents meant exploring the West Indian island of Guadeloupe! But I didn't see nearly as much of my brother as I would have liked.

Letters and postcards arrived – a typical one came from the Gambia, and reads: "Dear Sheila and Ron, It was very pleasant spending the weekend in Suffolk with you – almost a month ago I suppose. It doesn't seem that long. I'm in transit from Dakar to Mauritania, but have to stop over here because relations between the two countries are so bad that there are no direct flights. With luck I shall continue tomorrow, although this place is crawling with African heads of state, which is always disruptive. I was most relieved to find that I still had a room at the hotel. Lots of love, David."

Moving around, usually with accommodation provided, David and Nicole did not own a home of their own for many years. Around 1980 he wrote saying he felt it was time he acquired a base for his family, and asking me to look round Suffolk for a Tudor farmhouse with a large garden similar to ours. I was thrilled with the prospect of having my brother and family as neighbours, for once not merely in the same country as us, but in the same county! There is nothing I enjoy more than investigating ancient country dwellings, so we got in touch with local house agents and started having fun. Soon we discovered a beautiful un-restored farmhouse, heavily timbered and near a pretty village. We were all ready to take the next step – when I received another letter from Botswana.

Now, Nicole was brought up in warm, sunny climates and finds England damp and chilly. So there had been another family conference, and a change of plan. France was now the chosen location. David asked, were we interested in going halves

Bordepaille, near Monsegur, south east of Bordeaux

with them and buying a place in France together?

Well, of course I was interested! But we had no money. My brother never understood how short of funds we were while our seven children were young and we had only one wage coming in! So reluctantly, we said "Thanks, but no thanks". Very soon, a friend of Nicole's provided particulars of a stone farmhouse south east of Bordeaux, standing in ten acres and looking totally delectable with its shutters and quaint *pigeonnier*. Sight unseen, it was purchased. Of course, agents' photos do not tell the whole story and a mountain of work awaited them. We had made the right decision in letting this "opportunity" slip through our fingers and not sharing the purchase.

Naturally, we had to visit as soon as possible, and next summer we trundled through France in our dilapidated van (no windows or seats in the back) loaded with supplies, holiday gear and children. We found the remote location, and in trepidation picked our way over rubble and hunks of timber, shining torches downwards so that creepy-crawlies scuttled into the dark corners in a panic. Wondering what daylight would reveal, we clambered up rickety wooden stairs to dry quarters in the *grenier*, where we spread out our sleeping bags beneath the cobwebs.

We had arrived before my brother and his family, and as "rent" we re-painted the flaking shutters. David had asked for green. The paint was a little dark, so we mixed it with white – hey presto, a startling shade of duck-egg blue! Undeterred, we brushed away and these shutters were proudly displayed a few days later when my brother and his family joined us. Afterwards it seemed to me that we had set a trend throughout the land, as we would drive south noting how popular duck-egg blue shutters appeared to be!

The years slipped by, we all grew older, children began to leave home. I knew my brother often lived on the edge of danger, I knew he had capsized while sailing in the Indian Ocean, that he camped out in lion country, that he explored dark volcanic hills on foot, knowing that in many areas the natives are NOT friendly and when traffic accidents occur, have been known to emerge from the bush and stone the injured! But somehow I thought he would always survive, he would always be there for me, and one day when we were both old, grey, and retired, we might at last spend more time together.

During the months when I was hunting for a French retreat, I received several letters from David. In one, he tried to persuade me not to buy, and to simply continue enjoying his French hospitality. In another, he gave advice on conversion of currency, French banks, and so on, even offering to write a cheque for my deposit if that would help. From afar, he closely followed our progress.

On Easter Day 1997, in Suffolk, we were about to sit down and enjoy an enormous turkey with some of our family, when the phone rang. It was my sister Margo, in Devon, telling me David had been killed that morning in Chad. He had gone for a walk, to see what was going on in the primitive township where folk struggled to survive. A smuggler pursued by police, driving a stolen wreck of a car, swerved, hit David headlong, and careered onwards. Poor Nicole, hearing the bang and the commotion, wandered outside curious to see the cause, and found her own beloved husband dead in the road.

I was stunned with shock and horror. I could not believe it and yet I could not stop crying. My handsome brother David, with his lovely golden hair and his laughing blue eyes – it did not seem possible.

That day we had with us, younger daughters Elisabeth and Juliet, son Jim, and son David with his partner Jane. The plan had been that after dinner, Ron, Jim and I would leave for Prague (in the van of course, which this time was loaded up with furniture) as Jim was going out to live with his girlfriend Martina, and wished to introduce us to Martina, and to her fabulous home city. In a moment, all this was changed. I could not go to Prague; I had to go to my Mother, who would be as desolate as I and who would need comfort. So our journey detoured to the extreme north-east of the London Underground, where I waved a tearful goodbye to Ron and Jim as they headed for the East Coast ferry.

The journey down to Devon was surreal. Due to repairs, many trains were replaced by buses, and stations seemed bereft of staff who could explain the route. Crowds of bewildered people stood on platforms, suddenly surging like a tidal wave onto other platforms as trains were heard arriving. I felt strangely comforted by the fact that nearly all the other passengers were black; these were the race who had surrounded my brother in his last days and weeks of life. He had been touring the dry land of Chad, trying to select worthy projects to be funded by the World Bank. To quote from some of his last letters:

"Today we visited schools in Sarh, a town that has seen better times. The schools were a bit of an eye-opener; the 'Ecole du Centre Culturel' was built entirely of grass mats, and the children sat on little piles of broken bricks or broken car batteries. The teachers are paid between seven and ten pounds a month (less than a tenth of what we pay our cook, but then he is better educated than most of the teachers!). The worst school had 230 filthy tiny tots squatting on a mud floor in rags, supervised by a man with a whip, and occasionally erupting into surges of fighting. I called it the *'poulailler'* (chicken coop), and the name has stuck. I was able to find one child who could recognise the letter 'a', but nothing beyond that.

However, the encouraging thing is that in most classes one finds at least one child who has really learned something and can read without stumbling, or do simple arithmetic. The best school by far was an old one built by missionaries (now long-departed), in a half-Christian village. We even found one well-dressed woman with the rules and regulations of the sewing club!... Our house is on the banks of the River Chari... there is constant river traffic to and fro just by our house, much of it smuggling, but some of it just ordinary ferry activity. I am very tempted to take a ride, but I'm afraid I might be arrested as an illegal entrant to Cameroon on reaching the other side..."

That was a dreadful day. But there are some moments I will never forget. My "children" who didn't know how to make things better for me, decided to clean all my windows. How kind! I am no sort of housewife, so it is a treat for me to receive help; and it gave them something practical to do. For me on that day, nothing seemed to have any purpose any more, and I realised quite clearly, for the first time, that a major part of the pleasure of owning my French *fermette* was the delight of showing our achievements to my brother, and of discussing with him the many possibilities. Suddenly I couldn't see the point of owning the *fermette* any more. This feeling passed – after all, so many other people have enjoyed sharing our venture – but it is one of the memories of that terrible day.

The last time I saw my brother alive was at Pradelette. He and Nicole turned up un-announced in August 1996. Typically, David set to work instantly. Ron was having a battle with some recalcitrant plumbing. David drove off with him to the *quincaillerie* in Châtelus, to root out the correct bits and pieces using his knowledge of both the French language and the idiosyncrasies of French plumbing. He would not sit down for a meal until the problem was sorted. He was a wonderful brother to me, and so skilled in so many areas.

Of course our next visit to Pradelette was tinged with sadness. I found myself telling all the neighbours, tears once more streaming down my face. As always, they were so kind and *sympathique*. Andrée even sat down and stitched a beautiful frilly cushion for me, as a present to cheer me up! David had chatted in his friendly way to most of our neighbours the previous summer. He will not be forgotten.

How many faces there are to life: tragic, happy, comical, curious, sometimes unbelievable... this sad event brings to mind certain strange coincidences that at one time looked like becoming totally unbelievable. I will explain: right from early childhood, I had dreamed of having a huge family of children. We made a good start with seven. While mine were still young, my sister and her husband were working in the Congo as medical missionaries. They asked me and Ron if we would formally agree to become guardians of their children if she and her husband were to die. We said yes. My brother David and his wife Nicole, later asked us the same question – and so did my childhood friend, Ottilie. Each time, we said yes. We felt quite safe... friends and relatives don't die, do they?

The years went by. Margo had two boys, two girls. David had two boys. Ottilie had two girls. Then it started to happen; Ernest, husband of Ottilie, was killed on his motorbike. His children were aged nine and eleven. Margo's husband died of cancer – their youngest, Jonathan, was eleven, and all four were still at school. I began to have a spooky feeling – were Ron and I destined to end up as parents and guardians to fifteen children?

It did not happen. Of those three partnerships for whom we were to act as guardians, only the women remain. All the fathers have passed away. I feel so lucky myself. My dear husband is still here to share the grandchildren and the peace of the countryside on both sides of the Channel.

20

NIGHT LIFE

"WE'VE done nothing but work for two whole days. Let's get smartened up and have a night out!"

"OK, I could do with a change, too. It's a funny sort of holiday mixing cement all the time!"

"Where shall we go? Let's try Boussac – there's sure to be a night-club or something."

Stephen, our son (usually known as 'Diddy') and Andy (friend and builder) had a rapid wash and spruced themselves up. Full of eager anticipation of the high life, they drove off into the starlit October night. It was just eight o'clock.

To our surprise, they were back soon after ten.

"You're early, what went wrong?" we cried.

"Well, we drove all round Boussac and everywhere was shut up, nothing happening anywhere. So we drove all the way to Guéret and went up and down the streets looking for some sign of life. We finally found this pub. Nothing much was happening, and everyone went home before ten o'clock!"

Some of our visitors arrive with ideas of brilliant evenings to be spent in exciting bars, cafés and night clubs. "In your dreams!" We say. July and August are the months for evening entertainment; afterwards life goes back to normal. Many folk are in bed by nine, where some of them watch television in comfort. We see the changing lights through the curtains. No doubt they get up equally early (but I am never around to see – for me an early morning is being ready for the bread van at eight-fifteen).

So where could we go in the evenings? Our neighbours told of Scrabble Evenings in the little Village Hall, and meetings of the *Troisième Age* Club (over-sixties). Then there were the fishing competitions at the artificial lake – but none of these quite fitted the bill.

We had often remarked on a small hostelry at an isolated crossroads two miles from the village. Here beer adverts swing from trees, which shade an array of battered white plastic tables and chairs. Often flocks of cumbersome muscovy ducks are perched on these – we never saw people. But lights were on in the house some evenings, something must be going on. So one night we plucked up courage to knock at the door.

Surprised faces stared at us, but Madame politely invited us in. We were in a small kitchen. A few wooden chairs stood around the walls, and on these sat half-a-dozen raincoat clad men of indeterminate age. Two or three of these stood up and shuffled out as soon as we were through the doorway. We were a mixed party, and I think we females were regarded as intruders in a male domain. However the remaining clients welcomed us with shy smiles and we sat down around a small oil-cloth covered table. We ordered beer and lager, which Madame obtained from a cabinet in a passageway, finding us glasses from the draining board by the old sink. The mantelpiece held an ornate clock, and there was a charming display cabinet on one wall, but otherwise, this was a plain, simple kitchen. There was no bar.

After explaining who we were and where we were living, conversation trailed off. One of our party, Chris, spoke fluent French, having been billeted in Paris after the war. So we tentatively embarked on a discussion of "what I did in the war". At first things were amicable and interesting. Then one of us mentioned the war career of an elderly local man we had met earlier. Voices and faces changed; we were on dangerous ground. These men did not believe the story – he had been involved in something shady, something collaborative maybe, we should not believe what he had told us. Factions emerged – there were more differences of opinion, there had obviously been a range of options locally and memories were long and unforgiving. The Vichy line runs through the Creuse. Long-ago suspicions re-surfaced: we had stumbled into a hornets' nest!

Nervously, we back-tracked and tried to change the subject. One shrivelled old man boasted that he was in his late eighties. He was tiny, and when he stood up to leave, he seemed no taller – at most, four feet six inches! A smiling little husk of a man, his raincoat belted with binder twine, he disappeared into the night, his friend supporting him over the step.

This was the signal for others to leave. We followed suit – it was nine o'clock, pumpkin time! Our hostess begged us to call again, so she at least had been pleased to see us. We did return, twice. We had learned our lesson: "Don't talk about the war". Even so each time, our presence seemed to put a damper on proceedings, and we never managed to find out which evenings the hostelry was officially open for business. In the end, it seemed politic not to go at all.

We did learn a useful trick from the wistful little lady who ran this bar. If a wasp came into the kitchen, she would light a gas ring on her oven, and turn off all lights. In the darkness, we would hear her counting to ten. Then the lights went back on, and hey presto, there was the wasp, legs in the air, dead in the middle of the table!

We have several times ordered a meal in advance at local bar-restaurants. The food is excellent and not expensive, also genuine. The succulent *coq-au-vin* was definitely not a factory bred, frozen bird. He was probably strutting his stuff only yesterday, we felt. On all these occasions, tactful tidying-up began around nine thirty and we tried not to outstay our welcome.

At one of these locations, our host was Gilbert, a saturnine man with cavernous black nostrils. I was mesmerised by these nostrils and had to make a conscious effort not to stare whenever he approached our table. His helpmeet was Elodie, a pleasant-faced, buxom blond in her early fifties. She confided to us that Gilbert was not good to her and she was preparing to leave him. She had found herself a live-in job miles away in a hotel. In a sudden rush of generosity she presented us with a gift, handling it with proud reverence. Graciously we accepted it. The label on the jar declared it was green tomato jelly. It was certainly a sombre khaki shade, but was not jelly – it ran like water when the jar was tilted. I have kept it, and examine it from time to time, unwilling to open it, and equally unwilling to throw it away. It was given in such a soulful manner.

French gossip is just as good as the English variety, and neighbours explained to us that Elodie was Gilbert's fifth wife. Somehow he sucked spouses in, then got them to do most of the work about the place and neglected them totally. His time was spent drinking and smoking with cronies at the bar. How did he do it, what was the attraction? I was mystified. But only a year later, sure enough Gilbert had another woman at his beck and call – *numéro six!*

Strangely in contrast to the early bedtimes of most Creusoise, when there is a *foire*, *feste*, or special display, the official starting time is exceptionally late by our standards, and the actual starting time may turn out to be even later. No one complains, everyone is very good-natured and out to enjoy whatever surprises are in store.

One year a drama was advertised, to be held at the top of the Pierres Jaumâtres hill. We climbed through steep chestnut

Pierres Jaumâtres

woods to reach the arena and buy tickets. Canvas changing-rooms had been erected, and fabulous costumes hung within. Artefacts of the period to be depicted lay around. These included ancient weapons, such as swords and a blunderbuss. Tiered seating faced the enormous rocks that would serve as stage. The story of *"Martin, Maçon de la Creuse"* would start at 10.30pm. Unfortunately, terrific thunderstorms prevented this performance taking place for two successive nights. We had to return to England, but left our tickets with other members of the family to enjoy. The next night, the weather was fine, the audience took their seats – and nothing happened until well after eleven o'clock! By the time the play ended (around two in the morning) the air was chilly and Jane at least did not know the outcome of the drama; she was fast asleep!

We are sometimes delighted to find free events taking place outdoors in summer. Firework displays are very popular. At Moutier d'Ahun we waited among a volatile chattering crowd for a celebration to begin – eleven o'clock on the posters, twelve o'clock in reality! There were many young families present, and the parents kept the young amused with hot-dogs and other goodies from the many stalls as they waited. The show, when it came, was magnificent, well worth the wait. Thousands of pounds worth of fireworks lighted the night sky above the old romanesque bridge. The Celebration was to commemorate the thousand years since the Abbey had been founded. Today only an elaborate arched gateway remains.

Another time we travelled a good distance south to see displays of traditional dances and unusual horsemanship. We were lost, we were late, we feared the show would be half over – but no, it hadn't even started! We had time to position ourselves in the darkness. Troupes of young folk draped in many-layered traditional country dress danced and sang round an enormous fire. Then rural marriage ceremonies involving bonfires were enacted. Couples, wearing long trailing garments, had to leap over flaming bonfires to cement the marriage. Miraculously, no one's clothes caught fire, but the grass did. At first we were not sure whether this was a planned part of the display; but the area under fire grew and grew, until organisers and dancers armed themselves with sticks and beat out the flames. No one seemed to worry unduly, and the audience moved en-masse, in relaxed manner, to another field.

Here, after another period of waiting, the amazing dancing horses performed tangos, waltzes and fox-trots. They pirouetted on tips of hooves. They lay down and "died". They carried jousting knights in armour. There was no end to their talents. The finale was a startling display of exploding rear-ends! Horses appeared, encased in medieval battle gear, ridden by knights in armour. With blinker-flaps over their bewildered eyes, the horses cantered one at a time before our spell-bound gaze, heavily draped in elaborate material to which scores of fireworks had been tied. Strapped to heads, necks, chests and backsides, huge batteries of rockets proceeded to explode horizontally all around the hapless horses. Maybe the horses were already deaf, maybe they were just well-trained and experienced – whatever, they endured the crashing explosions, the shooting stars and fountains of fire falling around them, galloping away into the darkness when all fireworks were spent. We had never seen anything like it.

Another event worth recording took place in late evening in the woods south of Guéret. The theme of this drama seemed to be elves, goblins, spirits benign and evil, who cast spells and curses on medieval shepherds and goosegirls. Love-potions featured, and there was much whimsical dancing under the trees. Best of all, I liked the moments when a sprite or a shepherdess would trip delicately to one of the trees, from which dangled various bits of ironmongery, metal triangles, tubular bells and gongs, on which they would perform a startling percussion recital. This seemed of symbolic significance; I couldn't follow the plot, my French is not up to it. But we were enchanted.

So, what next? We never know what to expect from Creusoise entertainments. We are rarely disappointed.

21

"NEUF JOURS DE FÊTE NON STOP"

"WE'VE worked like mad all week – when are we going to see some sights?"

"Today if you like, why not? I did see an advert in the bread van the other day – something about an 'Exposition'. I remember the big headline said 'Batteuse.'"

"What's that then?"

"Oh, I think it's some kind of traditional dancing, clog dancing I think..."

"Well that sounds OK, let's go. Where is it?"

"It said, at the Moulin de Fréteix. I'm sure I've seen that place on the map and it's not too far away. Let's go and look."

We found our precious large-scale map of the district and scrutinised it carefully. Yes, there was Moulin de Freteix, only about four miles away as the crow flies, but thanks to steep valleys alongside fast-flowing rivers, at least double that distance by road. We arranged to set out after an early lunch. Work togs came off, tourist-type gear went on, complete with straw hats and cameras. We found the place quite easily. It was reached by a narrow lane between cliffs and quarries where smooth rock in bright metallic hues was being cut. The road was packed each side with parked cars.

"It must be jolly popular, I've never seen so many cars all together in this part of the world,"

"Yes – better find a place to park and walk the rest of the way. Look, we're nearly there!"

"What a smashing place! There's cliffs on two sides, and the Creuse running alongside that lovely stretch of grass – and look, there's our neighbour Andrée! *Bonjour,* Andrée!"

"Goodness – isn't that Nicole and her daughter over there? Everyone seems to be here! Where's the clog dancing, then?"

"Can't see a stage... There's a whole lot of ancient steam farm machinery everywhere – look, that belt runs from the steam engine and makes all those other bits and pieces move. Clever, isn't it?"

Gradually we began to understand that *"batteuse"* meant "threshing machine". Brawny men straight in from the woods and fields watched in fascination as the ancient machinery creaked into motion, dust rising as the grain slowly filled a succession of hessian sacks. We explored the terrain, finding the mill-race and admiring the huge wooden water-wheel. The mill house itself had been converted into a bar and restaurant and was doing a fine trade. The far side of the field held a succession of little heaps of curios, arranged for sale on blankets on the grass. The vendors looked as individual as their wares; it was the French equivalent of a car-boot sale but prices were high. Everywhere, people were greeting each other, becoming convivial as the alcohol flowed, and steaming gently under the hot sun. We found a shady area near the cliff, where wild vines grew, and we could dip our toes in the fast-flowing waters of the Creuse. It was a blissful afternoon.

The pleasures and sights of the Creuse often take us by surprise, we are never quite sure what we are going to find. There is a lot happening in the summer

Exploring the ancient Abbaye Prébenoît

The château at Joliot

months. Every village has its festival, often with fireworks at night to round off procedures. Tourist Offices provide tempting booklets to entice us to new venues. Close at hand are "La Fée" (a statue of the Virgin surmounting a rocky hillside); also the *château* and a museum of rural life, in Boussac. A few miles beyond Boussac is Lavaufranche, a military garrison at which the Hospitaliers lived and worked, containing a large chapel with wall paintings and stained glass. Then there are the fabulous Pierres Jaumâtres, and the ancient Abbaye at Prébenoît, which hosts excellent art exhibitions throughout the summer.

We still discover new delights during every summer visit. To date, we have three times narrowly missed another spectacle most popular with our neighbours. This is, the July day on which hundreds of superb fattening cattle from surrounding farms are herded up the twisting lanes through the woods, and into the stony streets and squares of Toulx. Our neighbour Andrée tells us it is quite safe, spectators are seated behind strong rope barriers as the bewildered beasts thunder past.

Sometimes we are taken out by friends. Eric's family, who have an inherited weekend cottage at Domeyrot, invited us to a meal followed by a concert in the church. We were wined and dined in style. Porto-filled melon halves were followed by garlic salad, smoked meats, rich cheeses, pear sponge liberally doused in spirits and covered in cream – and all helped down by quantities of wine. Every time we were sure the feast must be at an end, another succulent course appeared. And then we were escorted, blinking, into the midday brightness to walk a hundred yards to the little church, and thankfully sit down to enjoy traditional music on lute, hurdy-gurdy, and small bagpipes. Of course, during the interval copious alcohol was to be served! We were glad the benches were hard and uncomfortable – that

Romantic
Villemonteix

might keep us from nodding off and disgracing ourselves! But we were glad to keep our sunglasses on even in this shadowy building, so no one would see our eyelids droop, and droop. What hospitality!

More populous areas of the Creuse (towards Limoges to the south-west, Montluçon and Aubusson to the south-east, and Lac de Vassivière further south) are a hive of tourist activity throughout the summer. The local paper, *La Montagne*, gives details of all the jollity, and the headline *"Neuf jours de fête non stop"* referred to one of the gigantic summer festivals of music and dance. These attract international professionals, and range from classical to modern, jazz to folk. But on the whole, we are very glad that "our" corner of the Creuse is off the beaten track – almost a time-warp as we wander along dreamy back lanes – and the entertainments and sights are home-brewed and very local in character. We love the atmosphere in our small rural neighbourhood, and hope it will never be "discovered".

22

HOME ENTERTAINING

"'ON they went, singing *Eternal Memory*, and whenever they stopped, the sound of their feet, the horses and the gusts of wind seemed to carry on their singing...' OK, everyone? Do you want it again? Right, here's the details. That's the opening sentence of 'Dr. Zhivago' by Boris Pasternak, translated from the Russian and first published in an English translation in 1958. It is a complex story of interwoven lives and loves spanning years before and after the Second World War. The main heroine is Lara. Now you have to write the closing sentence of the book... have you all got plenty of paper?"

Heads go down, everyone is either scribbling wildly or gazing into space. We shield our scraps of paper fiercely from the eyes of those around us. Five minutes later all is done, papers are folded and put into the little box held by Michael, whose turn it is to act as leader.

Michael now has to read out our efforts, and we each have to judge which is the true excerpt from the actual book. Points are given to those who judge correctly, also to those whose creative efforts were sufficiently inspired (or sufficiently clever, devious, or lucky!) to have deceived other players. This game is "Ex Libris", and it is our favourite game for playing on quiet indoor evenings. I am constantly amazed by the creative ingenuity of us pseudo "authors". The game is surprisingly difficult, since none of us has perfect memory for the beginnings and endings of classic novels. It helps if you know something of the plot and setting. But often, to me, the real answer is less convincing than some of the fabricated ones.

At home, if we have no meeting or other commitment to take

us elsewhere in the evenings, we tend to become zombies, slouch on the couch, and gaze mindlessly at whatever is on the small screen. When our eyes finally glaze over we give in and go to bed. At Pradelette, it is different – no television! Also no phone, no one can call us for a chat. No piano, no sewing machine, no hobby materials. So unless we busy ourselves, we are in danger of going to bed too early and waking up several hours later to find it is still dark outside.

Sometimes we talk. Some family and friends have a store of tales to tell, like Chris, who will begin "When I was in old Cairo just after the War...." or "I was walking by the river in Budapest when I looked down and saw..." Chris, in his seventies, is now based in Vienna but has lived in many continents and constantly travels from country to country. He has a battered little car in which he travels slowly and thoughtfully when in Europe, never tiring of new sights, sounds and smells. I was enchanted by his simple answer one day, when I offered to wash some garments for him before he moved on:

"No thanks, I've got two shirts, one for travelling and one for when I get there!"

(I hasten to add he is always clean and tidy!).

My colleague Linda was not quite so enchanted during his visits whenever a friendly farm dog would approach him with interest and sniff around. He would say loudly: "It's my trousers and shoes... the dog can probably smell my Linda!"

The Linda he refers to is his own dog, left behind with friends in Vienna.

I received a letter after one visit in which Chris wrote to tell of his journey home: "When I left I drove over that strange countryside 'Le Morvan' and down into the wine area around Beaune. All those amazing superior vineyards – those *châteaux*, those little villages full of little wine firms (in buildings very like yours), such amazing expertise which amazes me because I can't tell one wine from another. One old chap was dead sure he could tell the wine of his village from that of another three miles away. Maybe what they do to make the wine is more important than just where it grew. Then I went on to Switzerland, and so back to here, a bit worn out, but cheered by seeing so many fine things. Next week off to Budapest, and then off to California to help my sister. All the best, Chris."

How else do we entertain when conversation fizzles out? We sing, we play instruments, but this is not everyone's cup of tea. We have played cards with French neighbours. We tried to teach them Canasta, which involved much talk about numbers, always a difficult topic, and at the end of the evening we still had the upper hand through not being fluent enough to explain some of the subtleties of play.

Our neighbour Andrée lent us her French version of Scrabble. This was interesting, since the number of tiles representing each letter is carefully adjusted for play in each language. Therefore, because for example French words use, on average, far more "U's" than English words, there are an amazing number of "U" tiles. Conversely, there are very few "W's". So using a French set is a challenge. One day we will experiment with bi-lingual Scrabble, I hope!

We love entertaining guests at the *fermette*, but for our immediate family, it has become a little more difficult for them to visit as the years have flown by. Most now have young children, and the journey is long and hot and difficult if packs of nappies and supplies of baby food are needed. Also we have in some ways made the place even less "safe" for youngsters than it was when first seen. Stairs with no banisters, unguarded upper landings, first floor rooms with missing walls! and so on. However we are delighted when they do come. Tom and Pauline were the first to bring little ones, Jessica, Helen and Ben. Tom was astounded by the size of our project, and suggested it might be more practical to sell half the building to a French family and just restore one half ourselves. I'd hate to lose any of it, and besides, in the Creuse there are more houses than people. Many of our neighbours have two or three houses to their name as a result of depopulation and the French inheritance laws.

Eating out

Our son Jim, with wife Martina and three year old Kuba
stayed over a week at the *fermette*. (They were in our power,
being on a car-less visit to us from their Czech home!) Kuba
enjoyed playing with Xavier and Jordane, grandsons of our
neighbours Nicole and Jean; and we were all entertained to tea
in the garden of Andrée and Guy. The French adore children, it
seems. We drove the family home via Switzerland, where we
stayed one night with Simone and Paul, who were our neighbours in Pradelette until the year 1999. It was a grand experience to be with them and their family in a summer chalet in the
high pastures, near Lac de Joux. They are in charge of a herd of
Holstein cattle, the dairy being under the same roof as their living quarters. I was amused when Martina asked me to tell
them that she could help with the milking if they would like
her to, because she once milked my sister's Golden Guernsey
goats. Martina was born and brought up in central Prague and
didn't even see a cow until she was fifteen. She honestly
thought this herd would be milked by hand. The next morning

I met her in the milking parlour in the early hours (the sound of the steriliser and machines woke us all). Martina was awestruck by the number, and sheer bulk, of these gawky cattle seen at close quarters. The bull was also loose in the dairy, keeping a wary eye on us and on his ladies!

Simone and Paul showed us cellars full of museum items – huge vats and presses for cheese making. Their bedroom is directly under the roof, alongside the *grenier* full of hay. A trap door here allows hay or straw to be dropped directly into the milking parlour. A ground floor door leads from kitchen to parlour. We ate meals with the family on a covered verandah with barbecue. A row of gigantic cowbells filled an entire wall – these were trophies from agricultural shows of former days.

We miss Simone and Paul at Pradelette. They were ever helpful, giving us a great deal of building stone, and often inviting us round to their farmhouse in the evenings to watch television or play music. But we now have new friends next door, Olivier and Liliane, who work immensely hard with their large flock of ewes. We can sit on our *terrasse* in the summer evenings, and watch them training up their eager young collie sheepdog. Some evenings we are able to admire the skill of Liliane's mother as she wields sickle or scythe around the young fruit trees.

On chilly spring or summer evenings it is good simply to sit around our open fire. We may roast chestnuts, or ring the changes by cooking potatoes or sausages in the hot embers. One year a great deal of heating and bending of metal took place around this fireside in the evenings. It was a challenge "forging" hand-rails for new steps. We watched in admiration as Michael carefully fashioned his grand chandelier in the embers.

To return to the subject of visiting relatives. In July 2001 our friends Elizabeth and Graham were staying with us. Belatedly, Ron and I realised it was our forty-second wedding anniversary (we are equally bad at remembering, so no one's feelings get hurt!). Graham insisted on treating us to a meal. So we sallied forth to "Le Moulin de Freteix", that delightful small restaurant tucked away in an idyllic corner right on the banks of La Petite Creuse. Returning home, to our astonishment we saw lights in our *fermette*. Entering the lighted kitchen, I heard a tiny voice from under our kitchen table (covered with a red-and-white plastic cloth which hangs down all round), saying: "Where's my umbrella? I know I had my umbrella! Where has it gone?"

Out popped a little dark head in a pink crocheted hat. It was grand-daughter Amy, aged three, very preoccupied with the lost umbrella. What a lovely surprise! In the back garden we discovered her parents David and Jane erecting their tent before nightfall. They had no idea it was our wedding anniversary, but their arrival made a special day even more special.

We hope visits from all and sundry will long continue, and as the years go by maybe we can entertain in greater comfort and style. Thank you all for coming.

23

CREUSOISE CREATIVITY

"WHAT do you think of this one? It's a kind of slug with legs, isn't it?"

"Possibly – but maybe it's a bit pig-like too, look at that snout!"

"Let's go round the corner. Look, that's the best yet – it's a kind of dragon or crocodile, or possibly a frog with those bulging eyes!"

"Isn't it a bear? Those bumps are ears, not eyes, surely?

"Oh yes, I can see that now. The man sitting near him looks so calm and sedate, so normal, doesn't he?"

"Yes, he's very watchful though, meditating perhaps – it must be quite spooky in these lanes at night, with all these weird creatures looming up in the dark."

"What about this one – is it a mermaid? It's got a kind of double pair of wings, or they could be fins for swimming."

"Mmm. . .it must have taken ages to carve it, it's huge and really detailed. Where on earth do you think he got his ideas from? Maybe he just started from the shape of the stones he was working. They're peculiar, but it really makes you look and wonder, doesn't it?"

"Yes. You know how the French love eating different fungi? Well, I wonder if the artist was on magic mushrooms or something?"

We were admiring the village of Masgot,

home of sculptor François Michaud, who lived and worked there in the nineteenth century. It was a hasty visit, as we had arrived late in the day, after a long tour of various places of interest. The custodians of the village and its museum were getting ready to close, but we had a quick peep into the museum and the workroom where today's would-be stonemasons and sculptors can learn the basics of these crafts. We took a handful of publicity material and left, vowing to return for a proper visit one day in the future.

Reading the brochures with the help of a French dictionary later that evening, I was surprised to learn that among Michaud's interests were humanism, mysticism, pre-Marxist socialism, Buddhism, and the search for a utopian way of life. He had anarchist friends. I wondered how it came about that a man born and bred in an out-of-the-way village, hidden in deep forests, living in the nineteenth century, had such a broad perspective on life. Masgot seemed so remote, just one among many scattered hamlets where no-one had much money or schooling.

Back in England, I settled down with piles of tourist brochures and my "Atlas of World History" to find out more. I read of a chaotic series of events in central France over the centuries. The following is a brief summary.

There is a rich, diverse heritage in the Creuse due to the presence of human beings over thousands of years, influenced by a tremendous variety of incomers, creeds, and cultures. First, pre-historic man; the cave paintings further south tell something of their lives. Then came pagans, Druids and

Celts. These were joined by evangelists sent by the Pope, as early as 250 AD. Best known, probably, is St. Martin of Tours. He came from a warrior family but to their bewilderment, became a pacifist. He is reputed to have torn his uniform cloak in half one day (while still a cavalry man) in order to share it with a naked beggar. That night he had a dream in which Christ appeared to him, dressed in this piece of rich material, saying "my friend Martin gave me this gift". Martin was converted to Christianity by this vision and many are the holy buildings bearing his name.

The Christian religion was diplomatically grafted on to existing beliefs in the region, never quite supplanting them. Thus, magical healing *sources* became holy wells or healing springs, blessed by the Virgin Mary or other saints. Sacrificial altars and standing stones acquired added significance without losing their original identity in the minds of local people. As late as the 17th century, occasional "black masses" or curses were endorsed by so-called Christian *abbés*! (In our home village in Suffolk, the last "trial by water" of a man suspected of witchcraft took place in 1825, when an unfortunate elderly man was tortured for hours in the cold waters of the village pond. The local clergyman put an end to proceedings). In the Creuse, happier magic still holds sway, with the sprinkling of salt and gathering of wild flowers to bring good fortune. These flowers had to be picked before dawn, with no witness present; and the picker than had to walk backwards out of the field! Dried flowers still hang over fire-places to bring good luck.

The days of the Roman Empire were succeeded by invasion by Huns, Franks, Vandals and Visigoths. The usual European mix of conflict, defeat, ascendancy, oppression and subservience to various over-lords or branches of the Church went on through the centuries. Crusades, civil war, fights between nobles or claimants to the throne of differing beliefs, warring popes, and rule by English kings followed. Richard the Lionheart and the Black Prince made violent forays into central France. Later came Renaissance, revolution and the Republic.

In the twentieth century, many thousands of Creusoise men perished in the 14-18 War, and in the next war the Vichy Line separated the district from occupied France to the North. All history went into the melting pot to produce the artefacts and architecture we see today.

We may visit rugged fortified *châteaux* such as Boussac on its towering cliff; other *châteaux*, such as Villemonteix, tell of cultured nobles living a life of leisure, and still other *châteaux* are a harmonious mix of the two. Mixed history is all around. A good example is the Commanderie at Lavaufranche. This had a triple purpose – religious, defensive and agricultural. It was a stronghold of the "soldier-monks", the military religious orders. First came the Knights Templars, succeeded by the Hospitaliers of St. Jean, and lastly the Order of Malta.

The story of the Knights Templars says a lot about human nature. They started in the year 1118 as a religious order whose members (all noblemen) took vows of chastity, poverty and obedience. They were governed by a Grand Master. They built churches and hospices. But their main aim was to defend the Kingdom of Christ, especially Jerusalem. They soon became one of Europe's most powerful secret societies and therefore a threat to authority. They were eradicated by Philip the Fair of France around 1320.

Hospitaliers and Templars had ten bases in the Creuse. Most had a garrison, a lodging-house for pilgrims, a hospital for the long-term sick and a flourishing farm. Today at Lavaufranche you can see remains of the *pigeonnier* and nostalgic reminders such as domed basket-weave beehives, as well as beautiful frescoes in the chapel.

The geology and geography of the Creuse cannot be separated from its culture. The granite outcrops, patches of poor soil, and hilly terrain made both farming and building arduous. The strong practical buildings embellished with carved and dressed stone symbolise the spirit of a hard-worked people who appreciate beauty and have great originality. Sometimes decorations are in carved wood, as at Moutier d'Ahun where the church is an Aladdin's cave of artistry. Foliage, barley-twist columns, mythical beasts and two-headed monsters mingle with saints and martyrs. If you are surprised by these snarling grotesque creatures in a church, remember the prophecies of Daniel and the Revelations of St. John! The artists had fun (we have monsters carved in wood, gargoyles, Green Men and wodewoses carved in stone, in our Suffolk churches too). The strange creatures of Masgot village are not too different from those found in churches. If you want to delve even further back in time, museums hold artefacts from pre-history, and enormous amphorae (tall two-handled earthenware jars with a pointed end which could be stuck in the ground or stacked on shelves) left by the Romans. They stored grain, wine, oil and many other foodstuffs in these.

The hills of the Creuse have been mined over at least two thousand years, for fine white clay, tin, lead, gold, copper and quartz, and in recent times, even uranium! Examples of very early enamelled ware (10th century) have been found. At Lavaveix is an old coal-mine, and many quarries excavate stone and other building materials.

It has been said that in the Creuse, granite is king. Certainly, it is everywhere. It gave rise to another source of income for the area; the Creuse did not just supply raw materials, it supplied skilled building workers. As early as the 10th century migrant workers tramped the roads to sell their skills all over France. The movement grew over the centuries, until by the nineteenth, armies of men and boys tramped the roads carrying their tools of trade. Many were gone from March to November, leaving the women, children and old folk to cope with the livestock and crops.

There has recently been a re-awakening of interest in these workmen. There is an "Association of the Maçons of the Creuse", based at Felletin. The group encourages preservation and restoration of traditional buildings and the characteristic style and techniques. They aim to make known the role these maçons of the Creuse played in the history of building. Famous

The Creuse maçons built their farmhouses snug against the weather

names from the past include Gabriel, Sylvain, Amedee, and Martin Nadaud, who lived from 1815-1898 and whose centenary we narrowly missed celebrating at the Pierres Jaumâtre, thanks to thunderstorms which put paid to any outdoor theatricals.

The booklet of the Association explains how these workers – masons, stonecutters, carpenters, tilers and decorators – left the villages of their birth annually for "months of labour, suffering and grief." I hope they also had a sense of achievement and money in their pockets when they came home! They are said to have created many fine buildings in Paris, among them Notre Dame, the Tuileries and the Louvre. (Expertise and knowledge did in fact move both ways since Eiffel designed at least two viaducts in the Creuse!)

These workmen were powerful political activists during the 19th century. Their story was told by the famous Martin Nadaud, at one time Deputy of the Creuse, in his book *"Mémoires de Leonard"* covering the years 1830-1848. There is also a celebrated and lengthy ballad, written by Jean Petit, also known as Jean de Bouiex, which can be purchased printed on cloth. I have translated some of the verses below. The translation is very free so as to make the lines rhyme!

Song of the Maçons of the Creuse

Many songs are written
About all kinds of things,
Of happy boys and maidens,
Warriors, shepherds, kings...
Hoping not to bore you
I'll sing a song that stirs;
Friend, this new song praises
The *maçons* of the Creuse!

See how they tramped away
Upon their brave campaign.
Off they went to Paris,
To Burgundy and Champagne...
They are proud; remember,
If they have calloused hands,
It's just because they work so hard,
These *maçons* from our lands.

Behold, the gracious Pantheon,
The wondrous Tuileries,
The Louvre and great Odéon,
Palace of Industries...
All this grand magnificence

146

Brings glory to our land.
France owes these famous buildings
To the noble Creusoise band.

The author of this song
Claims no literary fame.
He's an apprentice Maçon
Who revels in this name.
He is content, a craftsman,
A happy life he's had.
He signs his name with pride
As a working Creusoise lad.

Certainly we owe much to the artists and stalwart builders who came before us. There's an endless feast of delight for visitors to the Creuse, and for those delighting in more refined work there are the tapestries, the stained glass, delicate lacework and the exquisite porcelain of Limoges. But my favourite aspect remains the sturdy earth-bound walls and farm buildings, and of course the self-expression set in stone; curlicues and saints carved in relief around doorways, and the enigmatic, comical beasts of Masgot. These all fill me with shame at my own inept efforts! What skill and pride other *maçons* brought to their labours.

Maybe one day I will redeem myself by studying methods and attempting a sculpture – or even, building a wall which actually rises at true vertical!

24

"BLESS THIS HOUSE"

A SINGLE-storey granite-built outhouse projects from the east wall of our *fermette*. The back part of this is curved, and encircles the bread oven. The front section looks like an ordinary lean-to shed for livestock – maybe goats or a pig occupied the lower half and the small shuttered hole higher up was to enable chickens to enter and perch on the rafters. Once there must have been a low loft-floor; the holes which took the beams are still visible.

During the early days of our restoration, when we had no drainage system or water, we had a makeshift chemical toilet in this shed. One morning I was sitting there, ruminating, and watching the shafts of sunlight streaming in through a row of small holes at the top of the little door. Suddenly, I saw a cross, very carefully measured out and carved as a gentle groove in the enormous block of granite on which the south-east corner of the *fermette* is built.

Since this cross is now inside the outhouse, I think the front or livestock-housing section of the outhouse was probably a later addition. The curved area behind it, housing the bread oven, was surely there from the beginning. I like to imagine those long-ago workmen taking time to create this cross, presumably seeking a blessing on their building and on the inhabitants of the *fermette*, and acknowledging their God.

Nearly a year later, as we scraped away ivy and various plant growth from the front wall, I discovered a second cross, on the other exposed side of the same cornerstone, that is, the south or front side. This set me wondering, and questioning. Jean-Claude, a French friend living in Bourges, told us medieval monks would inhabit village homes, from where they would bake bread for the whole village, and provide mass for the people on saint days and holy days. Well, this is possible, even if not probable! Our *fermette* is definitely the oldest in the village. At one time it was in prime position, with a view over the valley which slopes down steeply to the River Verraux, rising to wooded hills on the opposite side. At some later date, the newer farmhouse which now blocks most of this view was built parallel to ours, sixty feet or so to the south.

I had always been intrigued by the stone arch in the north wall of our big room, the original living room which has the fireplace. On the wall outside the arch is a projecting curved drain-stone with a groove for the water. There is a similar drain-stone opposite, on the south wall. This is where the low stone sink is positioned. So there was a sink, and opposite, under the arch, another place in which water was used – could it possibly be the site of an altar and piscina, I wondered? Again, probably not – but it is possible! To the left of this arch is the cupboard set into the wall, which opens in what is now the kitchen. The opening has an elaborate carved surround, not what you would expect to see in a room which was used to store apples, potatoes and similar winter stores. So we began to speculate – could this interior window have provided a meeting-point between monks and people? Possibly gifts for the holy men might have been placed here. We will never know.

The idea that this was a kind of shrine for past Christians pleased me, and I decided to try to recreate this earlier atmosphere. So one long winter, in England, I set to work painting "stained glass windows" showing scenes derived from ancient manuscripts and wall paintings. I had bought a small window for five pounds, in an auction. It had four large panes and these were each divided into four sections. I set to work painting (not proper leaded stained glass, I'm afraid, just painted glass, with a tube of thick black gungy oily stuff which is squeezed on to make outlines). One set of four is scenes from the life of Christ, one set shows the four Gospel-writers, another, early Saints

Shrine in village wall at Sous-Parsat

such as Stephen and Paul, and the last, later Saints and martyrs. Some of these are largely legendary, such as Saint Giles, sitting in his hermit's cave with his gentle white hind nuzzling against him. Another scene shows Anne, mythical mother of Mary the Virgin, holding the child Mary on her lap, while enfolded in Mary's arms is the tiny infant Christ who will one day be born to her. I chose the scenes for their endearing naivety – it would be no good my trying to draw life-like figures even if I were not trying to contend with a drawing medium that is a cross between black treacle and engine oil!

I had a lovely time making my window. It is destined to go at second-floor level, in the wall separating the two staircases, so it can be seen from either side. I have not yet decided which side of the house will have the mirror writing, for each picture has its title.

I colour-copied some ancient icons in faded shades of blue, red and gold. These were framed and placed in various niches and corners. Then our friend Patricia wrote a special hymn for the house, inspired by a similar hymn sung at her church in Sussex. This hymn will one day be framed and displayed for all to see. I thought of adding some photos or paintings of the *fermette* as decoration alongside the words, one day when inspiration comes upon me! Patricia's verses are at the end of this chapter.

It's quite a challenge! We would like all visitors to be aware of an atmosphere of peace and spiritual refreshment; but this won't be the case if the shower leaks, the lights fuse, and spiders hang over the beds! But we are working and hoping and doing our best to make it come true.

PATRICIA'S HYMN

On this house, your blessing, Lord,
May its doors be open wide
To your lost and lonely ones.
Will you meet them there inside?
May the windows bright let in your light,
May your warmth be in the fire.
On this house, your blessing, Lord,
May your will be our desire.

Of this house, your building, Lord,
May our tools cut straight and true.
Carpenter of Nazareth
Will you help in what we do?
And may every wall grow strong and tall,
For we labour not alone.
Of this house, your building, Lord,
Will you be the cornerstone?

Round this house, your growing, Lord,
May our fruit, our trees, our flowers,
Flourish with our sowing, Lord,
And your sunshine and your showers.
For your beauty there is what we will share
With our neighbours and our friends.
Round this house, your growing, Lord,
And your love that never ends.

In this house, your music, Lord,
And let joy be in our song.
As we sing, the rafters ring
With our voices all day long.
Teach us all your sweetest harmonies
So that cares and worries cease.
In this house, your music, Lord,
Full of happiness and Peace.

L'ÉGLISE

WHEN we are in England we attend the Anglican Church. Ron is organist and choirmaster and I am a Reader so we rarely miss a Sunday. In France we enjoy being able to sit back and watch others take the responsibility!

Creusoise churches are Roman Catholic – we have never seen mention of any other denomination. As in England, budgets are stretched to breaking point and in rural areas priests have huge pastoral districts to care for.

In Suffolk, even the tiniest villages have their own beloved parish church. In the Creuse, only the larger villages possess churches. These are well cared for despite being of great age. It is lovely to find the majority open throughout the week, apparently with no fear of theft.

The two priests in "our" area of the Creuse take services in about ten churches. Only the larger villages have a service every Sunday. Times and places vary week to week, so lists are displayed in each church porch. We study these lists carefully, hoping for the chance to visit new out-of- the-way villages and attend special services such as patronal festivals.

The atmosphere in these country churches is relaxed and informal. A wider cross-section of the population appears to attend than in Suffolk villages. Late-comers don't sidle in looking embarrassed; they saunter in confident of their welcome. This is lovely to see – the Church seems to belong to the people, even to those who come so rarely that (like us!) they can't find their way around the service book. And yet they believe what happens in the church is for them and is relevant to their lives.

We have been pleasantly surprised by the major role of women in these Catholic services. Invariably women welcome people in, read the lesson, lead the prayers, and help with the preparation of the mass. The atmosphere is calm. There is no haranguing from the pulpit. For the address, the priest sits to read from a booklet, thoughtfully, not declaiming or dictatorial. There's a good feeling of one believer quietly sharing thoughts with other believers, all equal, all in it together. We enjoy seeing the familiar phrases and stories (in French of course) in Bible and service book. It's easier for us to understand because we know the themes so well, and the spoken bits help our pronunciation.

We've experienced marvellous patronal festivals. They have an atmosphere of community celebration and fun. Stalls outside the church may sell symbolic aids, such as brightly coloured ribbons said to be of value when praying for a sick child. People jostle to buy them. The younger priest organises lively singing practices before the service, for the hoards of young children who crowd into the church eager to be part of it all. Then a rather tawdry but revered plaster saint will be paraded around the village and carried shoulder-high into the church for the service.

We have attended "First Communions" during May, at which all the small girls wear white, and all the children (boys as well) hold bunches of lily-of-the-valley picked in the woods. Every household seems to have a bunch of these fragrant flowers in their kitchen at this season, and even the office of our builder's merchant boasted a huge bowl of lilies!

I was very impressed and moved by the willingness of these children to answer questions during the service, and to offer suggestions for prayer themes. They seemed glad to respond and did not give the impression of having been primed beforehand (though no doubt they were well taught).

At regular services churches are usually only half filled, but special occasions seem to gain tremendous support. For the villagers, this is very much their church and their living faith.

Marriage, Baptism, and First Communions are still the norm for many families, although modern ways now reach even the remotest country areas so that having a "partner" instead of being married is becoming more widespread.

Some of the church buildings look forbidding from outside. Once inside, stained windows glow and decoration is elaborate and colourful. Saints in wood or painted plaster fill every niche. Ceilings are painted brightly to show blue skies, sun, moon or stars, or cherubs trailing swirling ribbons. The Virgin Mary smiles serenely, and Christ on the Cross looks down with compassion on his people. Everywhere there is beauty to rejoice in.

However there is one aspect in which our Suffolk churches win hands down. This is, floral decoration. Many Creusoise churches have artificial flowers only on ordinary Sundays. That would never happen at home! Also pipe organs are rare, and organists even rarer.

There are hundreds of ancient churches, crypts, bell towers, chapels full of sarcophagi (carved stone coffins) well over a thousand years old, and abbeys. I am no expert, but there are plenty of guidebooks available. One small village church warrants special mention, it is unique. This is the church at Sous Parsat. Every inch of interior wall is covered with startling modern paintings by Gabriel Chabrat. They are extraordinary emotive portrayals of biblical scenes. There is an aggressive fight between Good and Evil spirits, the Exodus, massacres and healings, the Flight into Egypt, the Last Supper, the Crucifixion – you can almost hear the weeping, wailing, and gnashing of teeth! Swirls of vivid colour, grieving faces and beseeching hands surround the viewer. It is an experience not to be missed!

Graveyards in the Creuse are to our eyes, weird. They are surrounded by granite walls and gates which are often locked (might the dead attempt escape? I would not like such a resting place!). They are paved, cobbled, stone or gravel underfoot; no restful trees or grass as in the peaceful Suffolk churchyards.

The memorials are in little metal booths like bus shelters, or in small glasshouses, exclusive to each family. To the uninitiated they could be taken, from a distance, for garden centres with a range of greenhouses for sale.

Despite appearing so unattractive to me, these graveyards are well loved and tended by the villagers they serve. Flowers are everywhere (real as well as plastic!). There is a wide assortment of memorial stones, plaques and carved crosses.

I prefer green, beautiful, natural graveyards. This is what I am used to. These French versions which to me

Crucifix at Ligondeix

look so harsh and stark, like scars on the gorgeous hills and woods of the Creuse, are no doubt equally revered locally. They are certainly much visited. I suppose it's all a question of tradition, experience and expectations. Maybe the wild flowers that grace our Suffolk churchyards would be viewed as signs of neglect by these folk. Their dead are well under control!

Before closing this chapter I must mention the wayside shrines to Our Lady, often with an offering of fresh flowers at her feet. Every village, however small, has a carved granite cross at some crossroads or on a prominent rocky outcrop. Often there is a cross by a village well. At Ligondeix, the cross bears the figure of Jesus; a stocky workman-like figure with elongated face and huge outstretched hands. It reminds me of the Easter Island carvings.

Clearly, for generations, the Christian religion has been part of the air Creusoise villagers breathe, always present and enshrined in stone throughout the beautiful Creuse. Long may it continue.

THE (SECOND) GARDEN

PLENTY has been written about ownership of second homes. There is another concern of course – second gardens. Thank goodness for the winter months, I say. If the garden were in rampant growth for twelve months of the year all would be lost!

I love gardens, especially natural ones full of secret places. We have a huge garden in Suffolk. Ron works tirelessly to produce vegetables, cut lawns and hedges. I'm all right on the ride-on if someone just explains to me, two minutes before I get on, how the controls work. It must be some problem with my brain that makes it impossible for me to remember from one time to the next! Mainly, my gardening consists of looking in dismay at the rising tide of ground elder and wondering why everything I plant either grows enormous or disappears. But our home garden is wild and wonderful; masses of aconites and snowdrops, followed by crocus, daffs and bluebells, followed by shrubs, perennials, rampant rambler roses and honeysuckle. These contend with various unstoppable wild flowers which I naively introduced and which now think the garden is just for them – mainly sweet rocket, honesty, campion, Indian balsam, white musk mallow, violets in many shades, and white comfrey.

I did not want to buy a house in France that had no garden – there were plenty such on offer, tucked in between other houses and fronting the road. Not for me – mine had to be in a green oasis, please. I got my wish. But knowing I can't keep on top of a garden where we live ten months of the year, I did not intend to fall into the trap of starting another flower garden so far away.

The land around the *fermette* was not a "garden" by any stretch of the imagination when I bought the house. It was a waste-high shambles made worse by the presence of numerous foreign (ha ha!) objects lurking in the long weeds. We did have a small clump of wildish apple trees on the west boundary, and several lichen-covered relics (apple, pear and plum) scattered around the land behind the house.

I decided to aim for grass, shrubs and trees, with climbers on the house walls. It has taken seven years to achieve more grass than weeds. Tons of stone have been heaved up from the land and used in *terrasse*, stairs or walls. Some pieces were enormous and were painstakingly levered from place to place. Now, when there is a lull in the work, an interesting pastime is to walk around the garden probing with a large fork and investigating hard places to see whether they are underground rocks yards across, or stones that can be dug out and used.

There was an overgrown hedge on the east boundary, between us and the road, made up of hazel, wild plum, bramble, wild grape, and a plant similar to Virginia creeper, all growing around, over and through an ancient granite wall. This has been tidied, kept and enjoyed.

We defined the two long boundaries (north and south) with binder-twine, stakes and the sweepings from the farm end of the *fermette*. These sweepings consisted of animal droppings and grain husks nicely mixed. I covered this with yards of black woven material to keep down weeds, secured with hunks of granite, cutting holes every yard or so for shrubs and trees. It was a matter of pride to me that virtually all these plants were from cuttings or seed, nurtured in pots at home and transported to France.

In front of the house I put buddleia, tree mallow, orange blossom (philadelphus); also rowan trees in the hope that their delicate leaves and slender shape would provide a screen, but not an unfriendly barrier, between us and our neighbours. To this collection was added hibiscus and laburnum seedlings given by neighbour Andrée. These plants had to take their chance, protected by plastic guards but left unweeded for long periods each year. Remarkably, most did not just survive, they thrived and are a mass of blossom for much of the summer.

The long rear boundary is planted with hawthorn, hazel, black willow, guelder rose, spindletree, field maple and holly. These are not cut into a hedge, just left natural, pleasantly irregular in height and habit. Seven years of growth means they have nothing to fear from even the most flourishing thistles and nettles.

In the grounds of the school where I taught, I had planted a lovely little larch sapling. In term time it was safe, but during the long summer holidays, two years running it was bashed, battered and broken (presumably by footballers). I decided to rescue it and give it a continental experience. It is now a graceful tree, twelve feet high and (I now notice!) heading rapidly towards the overhead wires. I planted one other "specimen" tree, a snowy mespilus (amelanchier) which has a mass of white blossom, followed in autumn by red berries and red-gold foliage. We also planted a fig, but it was not proof against the chilly Creusoise winter winds.

Our friend Alan, an expert on vines and author of several books on the subject, gave us four different vines for "front of house". Some took a little while to establish, but for three years now we've had bumper crops and the vines are up to the roof. They soften the stone walls and add interest to the lives of lizards and nesting birds. Unfortunately, as I've said, they also attract wasps and gigantic hornets, who have a host of nooks and corners to choose from between the stones, where they industriously construct elaborate nests. We put up jam-jar traps, jam being the best bait (far better than bought concoctions).

We are fortunate to have an ancient granite millet mill standing in an angle of our south wall. When I first saw the *fermette*, this mill, a cylinder of smooth dressed granite chest-height, all carved from one single block of stone, was entirely hidden by

The garden emerges

growths of bramble, elder and nettles which enmeshed the mill and grew right in to the stones of the house wall, no doubt enlarging the dangerous crack. What a discovery when this growth was finally cleared and the mill revealed – although it stood among heaps of loose boulders which were bit by bit used to repair walls and construct my famous stairs. This mil-let mill is a greatly prized treasure. Beside it we planted a glory-vine given to us by French friends. This vine is making slow progress up the front of the house, and adding to its charm.

I took surplus nicotiana seedlings from Suffolk one summer, and planted them in old cooking pots and pans. There is plen-ty of sun and plenty of rain in this hill village, giving us new self-sown seedlings each year with a lovely evening scent. I also planted mint and parsley in various ancient utensils. Some have flourished, some expired, and of course the parsley needs re-planting each year.

Ron battled valiantly with the "lawn". On arrival each visit,

I was forbidden to approach the house until he had strimmed a path through the waist-high weeds to a few of the doors. Bit by bit each visit, the jungle was vanquished. At last, after eight years, it is sufficiently subdued for us to ask our young neighbours Sandrine and Alexander to keep it mown for us as a paid job. Arriving at the house now has become a delight rather than an exhausting endurance test.

The new *terrasse* on two sides of the house is bounded by a new granite wall. Maybe in the future, we will add a few labour-free plants where wall meets grass, and at the side of the steps. I fancy variegated periwinkle, being a rambling unstoppable plant which is attractive even when not in flower. Catmint and marjoram, sage, and maybe some clumps of thyme, all would look great against the stone and would perfume the summer air. I am taking cuttings of evergreen honeysuckle to wreathe around the stark new wire fence which has appeared between us and our neighbours' garden; and one day, there may be Virginia creeper twining around the wooden supports that will be needed when gutters are added to the long north-facing roof. Time will tell!

Really this is such an easy type of garden compared with the hazards of flower beds. I wonder whether we should convert our Suffolk garden to French mode!

26

MONEY, MONEY, MONEY

"HEAVENS, this must be a mistake... Look at this bill!"

"Let's see – 1,919 francs. What's that in English money? Exchange rate's about nine francs to the pound now, so that's about two hundred and thirteen pounds. What's it for?

"It's the *Taxe d'Habitation* charge. I'm just looking to see how much it was last year. Oh yes, 297 francs, that's more like it, only about thirty-three pounds."

"You'd better write and ask what's happened then."

So I wrote to the officials in Châtelus Malvaleix asking what on earth had caused my *Taxe d'Habitation* (equivalent to our Council Tax) to shoot through the roof. The answer was not long in coming. I was told the increased amount was based on the details of building that I myself had supplied.

I wrote again, bewailing the unfinished state of the property, the damp earth floors, the dusty disintegrating walls, the lack of ceilings or roof linings, the dearth of interior walls, and so on.

"It is not finished!" I wailed.

"*Tant pis!*" came the reply (but not quite in those words!). The new charge was based on floor area of living space and on the number of windows, doors, sinks, toilets, washbasins and so on. The condition of the dwelling had nothing to do with it.

Defeated, I looked out the plans I had drawn and sent, when seeking permission for Veluxes in the roof, two new exterior doors and three new windows. I compared these plans with the meagre plans provided by the house agent. They were entirely different. The original plans showed only the east or "house" end. There was no mention of the "farm" end of the

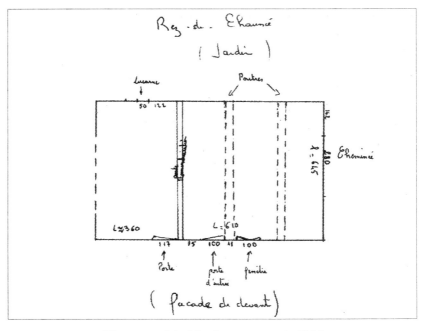

Plans provided by house agent, 1993

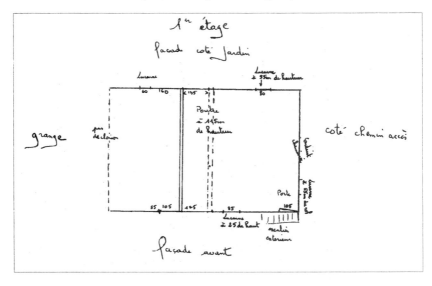

building. So that was only three rooms, none of which was in liveable condition when I acquired ownership. All had been dark, damp, with holes in roof, floorboards and walls, and half hidden under rubble.

Total floor area of these so-called "rooms" had been one hundred square metres. There had been no piped water in the house, the only supply being a mysterious pipe at floor level in the stable for use with livestock only; and of course, no drains.

I looked at the fairly honest plans I had submitted (see "Achievements" pages 66-67). We had to re-submit our application for permission to restore to a special department dealing with "change of use" because the former tractor bay, stable and grenier were to become residential accommodation. The apparent total living area was now two hundred and forty-six square metres; and I had owned up to one sink, one hand-basin and one water closet, plus septic tank drainage.

Since then we had installed a shower and a second toilet with hand-basin, but henceforth they would be my secret. I argued that since we were slaving away ourselves and making do with very rough and ready accommodation which could not possibly be rented out, officialdom should not have even more of our money. After all, I was doing them a favour really; how long would it have been before another nutty person came along to save this historic building from self-destruction?

On the plans I submitted, sneakily I had not made mention of my staircases. I was too afraid of a Stairs Inspector arriving to point out the uneven-ness of treads and risers and order their demolition. I had tried to make my stairs look old but had not entirely succeeded since no self-respecting French *maçon* of previous centuries would have built wavy lines from unshaped stone, as I had.

I then and there decided that all future alterations and additions would be interior ones. I would not ask permission for windows in the old *grenier* bedroom – the existing pigeon holes would have to suffice, becoming tiny peep-hole windows if and when we got round to adding glass to the tunnel-like apertures. My new grand front doors to the ex-tractor bay would live their lives behind the existing huge barn doors, which would act as shutters; so the front aspect of the building would remain unchanged. I was becoming ever more devious! But it was self-preservation really. We are an elderly retired couple after all.

Paying for an expensive fad like ownership of a second home is no joke. Of course it is an entirely unnecessary luxury. But when I am assailed with guilt for my self-indulgence, I hastily run through my mind the extravagance of others. What about people who own boats and expensive moorings? What about friends who go on world cruises or "pop over to Canada" for three days' ski-ing? What about neighbours who buy expensive four-wheel drives or sports cars every other year? There are so many ways of running through money and we neither smoke nor gamble (not even a Lottery ticket!). With these and other arguments I excuse myself and my folly.

Near our Suffolk coast we have village populations decimated through half their dwellings becoming holiday homes for the well-off, pushing up prices and limiting the choice for young locals wanting to set up home in the area. But this is not the same situation as in the Creuse, where empty and derelict dwellings are two a penny and vendors have to lower their prices to ridiculous levels to make a sale. Our neighbour Andrée recently sold a cottage dwelling she inherited in a nearby village, to a couple from Paris seeking a week-end retreat. The cottage had four good rooms, a sound roof, and a pleasant garden, and went for only 10,000 francs. We are told local councils are generous with permissions for restorations and alterations from "incomers", since the number of indigenous villagers is dwindling so fast. So I reckon I am really a generous benefactor, causing more folk to visit and re-visit the area and swell the coffers!

So, what does it cost to own this second home? Annual running costs hover around £500. Including standing charges for water and electricity plus the cost of water and electricity consumed, plus insurance premium, plus the two government taxes (Rates), bills in 1994 totalled only £163. Last year, 2001, they totalled £471 (of course the actual bills are charged in francs – or now, euros). This increase, expressed in the equivalent amount of sterling, is despite the fact that the exchange rate was only 8.5 francs to the pound in 1994, and at the time of writing was currently over 10 francs to the pound.

Purchase price with taxes and commission came to more than £16,000 due to the sudden worsening of the exchange rate at that moment in time – only 8.5 francs to the pound whereas it had been 12 a few years previously and is now again well over 10. Maybe the euro is not such a bad idea after all!

Repairs and alterations, so far, have been another £14,000 to date. Spread over eight years, perhaps this is not too bad. And one happy day in the future, maybe we will be ready to let our *fermette* to others who wish to enjoy the ambience of the Creuse. They will have to be folk who enjoy a flavour of the past – luxury mod-cons do not feature in our plans, even could we afford them. After all, luxury holidays are now run-of-the-mill, while we offer something distinctly different! The coast of much of the Mediterranean, and other coasts further afield, are spawning hundreds of high-rise white boxes of smooth flowing "plastic" profile, in which air-conditioning and central heating are automatic and all services can be obtained at the push of a button. As a tourist, you can wake up in the morning and not even know what country you are in – marina, golf course, pubs and clubs – same old routine. We, on the other hand, will be offering a more individual experience with echoes of the past in a present populated by "real" country dwellers. There must be some eccentric souls out there to whom this will appeal, surely? (WRITE TO ME!!!)

I have summarised expenses to date. But this doesn't tell the full story, since I have not included our travel costs (which also increase steadily) reasoning that we would have gone on holiday somewhere each year even if I had not become a second home owner.

DATE	OBJECT	AMOUNT STERLING
1994	Purchase of *fermette*	14,667
	Commission and Taxes	1,853
1995	Building materials	
	and construction of window frames	1,000
	Labour (English builder)	580
	Digging *terrasse* (French builder)	756
1996	Building materials	378
	Labour and travel costs (English builders)	685
	Second-hand doors, windows, sanitary ware	325
	Septic tank installation (French builder)	1,674
	Repair to mains pipe	129
	Reconnecting mains water	201
1997	Building materials	360
	Installing 3 doors	
	and 3 windows (French builder)	3,986
1998	Building materials	101
	Second-hand doors and windows	340
	4 Veluxes, and curtain poles	795
1999	Building materials	256
	Second-hand windows	30
	Installing 4 Veluxes (French builder)	450
	Purchase of 2 (more!) Veluxes	330
2000	Building materials	245
	Purchase of banisters and balustrades	214
	Making legal French Will	176
2001	Building materials	289
	Purchase of floor tiles	130
	Installing 2 Veluxes (French builder)	100

TOTAL COSTS of purchase and restoration 1994-2001   **30,050**

(...and it is nowhere near finished!)

When I was paying for the *fermette*, in 1994, I had no French bank account. I paid by Telegraphic Transfer Order (Telex Bank to Bank Transfer) at a cost of £28. Soon after, I acquired a Eurocheque Book and Banker's Card to support this. Only cheques for small sums could be made out, and for each one written there was a bank charge. So I used Eurocheques only in emergencies and this entire system has now become obsolete and been discontinued.

During our first summer visit, in 1994, I opened an account with the Crédit Agricole bank. This means I can pay bills received in England, for rates, insurance, water and electricity. I top up this account each year, using an English cheque written in sterling, and handing this in at Credit Agricole (there is a branch in Châtelus Malvaleix). Every time I top up my account in this way I incur bank charges. Since Crédit Agricole pays no interest on current accounts, I try not to leave too much money in, while at the same time being terrified that at some careless moment I will write a cheque that "bounces"! This is a criminal offence in France.

The greatest boon since owning the *fermette* has been my ordinary Visa credit card. This can be used throughout Europe in any currency at no extra charge. So of course I use it constantly, in preference to Crédit Agricole cheques, at garages and supermarkets and even at the builder's yard.

Now I await the changes that will come in 2002 with the euro. I have no "euro" cheque book yet. Hopefully it will all be made clear as time goes on. It's a shame really as I was just beginning to think in francs and once again I will have no idea how much I am spending when euros come on the scene. At least this situation enables me to be spendthrift without worrying when paying for restorations and materials. The currency feels to me like Monopoly Money and I splash it around with gay abandon.

Our *fermette* received some storm damage in December 1999. It took two years for me to sort out my insurance claim. Fortunately, we were told we could claim even for work done ourselves before my claim went in. This was great, as we spent many hours up ladders fiddling about with mortar balanced on a trowel. We claimed for our labour, at 60 francs an hour (I at least, am surely a much slower worker than any tradesman). So this was a welcome bonus and for once I was able to pay a French cheque into my French account (no charges).

A lot of headaches and mysteries will disappear if and when Great Britain adopts the euro. Apart from those moments of glee experienced whenever the exchange rate is in our favour, I think the euro cannot come too fast for me.

27

CREUSOISE LIVING TODAY

AS THE years have hurried by, we have evolved a steady pattern of visits to our corner of the Creuse – May, July or August, and October, are the months when we visit. Gradually a clearer picture of the place and its people has emerged.

Initially, I had a fanciful idea of what I wanted the place and its people to be – rural contentment and a life that has changed little in this era of so-called progress. I took note of scenes which reinforced my ideal, such as old men with buckets of water on the way to tend a house cow; front yards in which ducks waddle through puddles and mother hens cluck over chicks; old ladies carrying bundles of roadside greenery to feed their rabbits, or taking a doe-like goat with swept-back horns for a foraging stroll along the verges of leafy lanes. These all fitted my dreams, and were what I had hoped to see.

But although I saw all these scenes and more, they told only part of the story. Yes, in autumn dignified old ladies with baskets bend to pick up sweet chestnuts at the wayside, while stocky menfolk beat apple trees with sticks to loosen the last fruit. But this is not the whole story. Why should these people fit the pattern I had romantically adopted, for themselves and their lifestyle? As always, the picture is much more complex.

The Creuse is a depopulated area, now filling up with incomers such as ourselves, from England, the Netherlands, Germany, and elsewhere, with a scattering of Parisians who have purchased country cottages as weekend retreats. Still, the majority in the villages we know are indigenous Creusoise, and they are interrelated and intimately acquainted with the lives and histories of their neighbours.

An old man collects
water for his cow

Families are strong units. I have seen, and marvelled at, teenage children willingly helping their extended farming families – fetching vegetables in hand-carts from distant plots, riding on tractors, rounding up flocks and herds, or stacking heavy bales. But most families are decimated by their younger members looking for an easier, or more exciting, or simply different, way of life from the traditional one. Farming is hard: fields tend to be small and steeply sloped, often with rocky outcrops of granite. Our own *fermette* is built on one of these great solid immovable mounds. Bracken thrives in many meadows, which may have rocks in one part, and low marshy bog in another.

The modern world has made its ways known even here, and families send us greetings cards produced by younger members on home computers. Many roofs boast satellite dishes. Things are not always what they seem; I used to pass one farmstead in which the open front door revealed, even in August, a wood fire on which stood kettles and pans. "How quaint, how delightful!" I thought to myself – only to learn later that the husband is notorious locally for his meanness. Apparently he has plenty of money but is reluctant to spend any, so his long-suffering wife draws water from a garden well, washes by hand, uses an earth-closet and cooks on a wood fire. This is not her choice, they are not the norm!

Some of the things which most charmed me on first acquaintance are also not the norm. For instance, I loved to hear the cowbells on our local herd. Later I learned that these bells had caused great controversy in the village, as Paul and Simone, owners of the herd, are Swiss and had imported this Swiss custom which did not please everyone. One old lady in fact called in the Environmental Health Officials to record the level of decibels. This seemed strange to me, as to my ears much more obtrusive sounds were frequent, such as roaring farm machinery, or what we came to call a night-time "howling". This howling was quite terrifying on first acquaintance, sounding eerily like a pack of ravenous wolves encircling the village. Every household has at least one dog, or a pack of working dogs trained for *la chasse*. "Howlings" occurred in the dead of night; a single dog would start, joined one at a time by the competitive efforts of all other dogs within hearing – an unearthly, disturbing, primitive lament. Then, more suddenly than it started, the noise would stop dead and we could all go back to sleep!

My tentative suggestion that the tinkling of bells was much softer and more pleasant than other country sounds was dismissed. The animal sounds were "natural". The bells were "unnatural". End of discussion!

To return to the subject of family life. Creusoise families spend more time together than those we know in England. They visit more often, share meals, sit and talk for hours, and most notable of all, are good to their old folk. I have been in houses where the old mother or father obviously feels that they occupy a rightful place and are cherished and wanted. They sit at the table, slowly mumbling through hunks of bread with toothless gums, not hurrying, not fearing that they are an unwanted burden on the household, simply living at their own speed in a place that is home and will always be so. I wish that were still the English way!

I think one factor that leads to this willing acceptance of others is the French readiness to embrace and kiss at every opportunity. Kisses on the cheek are exchanged between old and young, male and female, at any time and in any place, without any trace of embarrassment. Young children offer their soft cheeks to older family friends and ancient bewhiskered aunts and uncles without any sign that they find this an irksome duty to be rushed or avoided. It is the natural thing to be close and to care for one another, in sickness or in health and whatever the situation. I think it gives people a warm feeling that they are part of a community and that they matter.

There are of course, other ways of being "natural". One that we can't help being aware of, is casualness about bodily functions! Slurping your soup at table is normal, so is wiping your mouth with the back of your hand. Public toilets are amazing – you may have to pass a completely open urinal in order to get to the female side of the convenience! At any large outdoor gathering, men will simply turn their backs and take a few paces away, to urinate, and this takes some getting used to.

Covered stone well at Ligondeix

I had an odd experience in the garden of an old man (now sadly deceased). He was very old, very deaf, and lived in an ancient granite dwelling with wooden ladder access to his upstairs living accommodation. When he descended this ladder, he would brush the odd cat or chicken from the rungs. I had several intriguing conversations with him, mostly (I think) on the subject of the war. One day I wished to talk to him, wanting to discover the ownership of a ruined cottage next to his home. There were gorgeous, shaped curved stone lintels over the gaping doorways, and since the roof was gone and trees grew high inside the walls, I hoped we might be able to purchase some stone.

Well, with this in mind I entered his unfenced garden, calling

"Bonjour, Monsieur". He saw me and descended his steps. He was holding a slab of butter in one hand as we drew near each other. Then, using the other hand, he started to urinate! I didn't know quite what to do – was it correct etiquette to pretend I hadn't noticed? Or should I carry on the conversation? Or should I simply turn away for a moment? I did none of these – I retreated rapidly and my question never got asked!

To return to more general matters – we have found the people of the Creuse friendly, considerate, exceptionally honest and generous. They are also hard-working, rising early to tend animals or crops. Even retired folk keep poultry, rabbits, and maybe a pig in the winter time. All have enormous vegetable plots in which hundred-yard-long rows of carrots, potatoes, turnips, cabbages, beans, cauliflower, tomatoes, and so on, run alongside each other with not a weed to be seen. Great stores of meticulously stacked firewood stand in most gardens, and in summer most households display blazing scarlet and pink pelargoniums and petunias on walls and in hanging baskets.

It is a delightful spot in which to unwind and enjoy the world. We are honoured by the welcome we have received.

28

A PLACE IN THE SUN

DURING Autumn 2001 in England, I became addicted to a series on television. Entitled "A Place in the Sun", it was transmitted every weekday at 5pm. I began to rush through preparations for supper, so that by the time the programme began everything was bubbling away nicely and I could just sit relaxed and enter a fantasy world.

The programme focused on English people who wanted to buy homes or second homes abroad. The countries covered ranged from Florida to Transylvania, taking in the Canaries, the West Indies and Turkey, as well as the more familiar second-home locations. What enterprise, and what bargains! I began to wonder why anyone was left in England with so much fabulous choice all around.

It was comical to see how the presenter geared her comments to the characters of the different prospective buyers. At one superb location in the mountains of Transylvania, the hopeful client commented on the lack of good roads in such a remote corner. "Oh," replied the presenter, "don't worry about that. They're building a Dracula Theme Park there in the next few years, that will soon put the place on the map!"

Horrors! That instantly finished Transylvania for me.

In an episode featuring Turkey, one village consisted of spectacular ruins over a thousand years old, on a lovely unspoilt stretch of coast. I was impressed that the Turkish government has strict rules about development in such an area. No new building is allowed, but people (including foreigners) are advised and helped if they wish to restore one of these roofless ruins in appropriate style. I thought it might be a little eerie to

At home

live in a restored house among so many empty stone shells. But I would love to see what has become of that village in ten years' time. Inland Spain and Portugal were interesting. I was fascinated by views of houses and mills constructed much like our Creusoise *fermette*, but on larger plots of land planted with ancient olive trees, figs, peaches, and even lemon and orange trees. Much of coastal Spain is horrific to me – hillsides awash with "villas" looking like show homes carved out of white icing, and not a native Spaniard anywhere (except perhaps those who do cleaning, cooking and gardening for the incomers).

Then there are the apartments and flats all around the Mediterranean, with golf courses, club houses, marinas, and use of shared pool etc. These are not for me either.

France of course seemed to have some of the most amazing bargains – old monasteries or *châteaux* with vast rooms, *maisons du maître*, mills alongside rushing rivers – many for the price of a semi in some parts of England. I was surprised how important it seemed to be, for most hopefuls, to have everything in sparkling tip-top order for them, without having to lift a finger. Some clients admired stone cottages, but recoiled in alarm at the possibility that a wall might need rendering or that the wiring was incomplete. Generally the standard of decoration and comfort was astounding – right out of our league. I was also a little depressed to see that in many areas of France, it is possible to buy a totally restored property about the size of ours, for LESS than our total costs to date! And we have done all the work ourselves, and we haven't even finished!

I console myself with the thought that our *fermette* is unique, and is becoming more so the more we work on it. So we'll keep going, and just make sure we enjoy every moment we spend in this district of charm and bonhomie. No time to dream – we must gird our loins and stick at it!

Bon courage! (Does anyone want to come and help us, please?)

29

WHAT NOW?

"WE loved it, what a beautiful place!"

"Aren't you lucky to have garden all round? It's so private, you're not overlooked by anyone. Even the house in front of yours has it's back to yours and is all shuttered up most of the time."

"The neighbours are really friendly – and we visited some amazing places – what was the name of that hill with the enormous granite boulders balanced everywhere?"

"We were astounded by all the work you've done – but we don't envy you the work that's still waiting!"

"What lovely little villages everywhere – we couldn't believe the prices at the house agents'. We even took a photo of the window display to prove it – so cheap!"

"We found a super café – five courses, only 60 francs!"

"Thank you ever so much for letting us stay there. We took loads of pictures, you'll have to come round and see them, and we'll tell you all about our visit!"

Neighbours Margaret and Roy had been our guinea-pigs. They were the first people to visit Pradelette in our absence, and they definitely enjoyed it.

It is eight years since I first set eyes on our *fermette* at Pradelette. We have come a long way since then. At first my intention was simply to enjoy the ancient building as a kind of camping base for holidays of exploration and discovery in France. But by rapid progression this changed to a desire to restore the place to a standard of comfort that would enable us to let it as a holiday *gîte*.

One reason for this change was Ron's desire to make basic

Farmhouse at Pradalette in 1996, drawn by Chris Taylor

repairs and keep the weather out to avoid further deterioration. He is very practical and just couldn't ignore the multitude of jobs crying out to be attended to. Thank you, Ron!

The other reason was rapidly escalating costs, as I have described in "Money, Money, Money". Also the improvements and restorations to date have doubled the original cost of the *fermette*. And now we are both pensioners!

We seem to have three choices:
- sell the *fermette*
- sell our English home and move to France
- or, make the *fermette* pay for itself

We're currently working on this last option! But will we ever achieve it?

I often wonder how I came to do something so crazy. I think it was the combination of desire and funds. There have been periods in my life when I have yearned to live on a Scottish island as a crofter... or to live right by the sea and keep a pack of donkeys for children to ride on the beach... or to become a craft potter or basket weaver... silly impractical dreams, that did not fit in with the needs of a large family; but dreaming didn't matter since there was no way I could do any of these things for real.

And then came a time when I was much more free to come and go, AND I had a little money – so it happened! It was a bit of a shock to me as well! And I have always had a niggling fear that the enthusiasm might evaporate before the project is completed. Thank goodness, so far I still have the energy and the urge to forge ahead.

There are dangers involved when you have the means to turn dreams into reality. I think about those who win the Lottery, and I don't envy them. There are several reasons why I have never bought a Lottery ticket. The first is, that I disapprove of the Lottery because so little goes to good causes and so much to the winners. I would rather see more, smaller, prizes and much more given where it is needed. The second reason is, that in my opinion winning huge sums of money turns lives upside-down and can even wreck people. Think of the temptation to buy everything you've ever wanted, all at once! What would be left to strive for? And what about the pangs of conscience if you find yourself too self-indulgent and too weak to give good-sized donations to charities who desperately need it? What about the jealousies and resentments among family and friends if you give different amounts to different folk? The possibilities fill me with terror!

I do have some guilt about having expended so much time, money and energy in such a self-indulgent manner when there is so much need in the world. But I console myself with the thought that we are saving and preserving something special and remarkable which will be enjoyed by many other people. We are also bringing people and funds to a disadvantaged corner of France, a Department whose population of 600,000 in 1960 had dropped to 300,000 by 1990, and to 124,000 by the year 2000. Our French neighbours seem to delight in our presence – we are a source of endless interest, and no doubt amusement. We give them something new to talk about, and as Andrée says *"Il me donne plaisir!"* when she sees our lighted windows at night, instead of living next door to a neglected and abandoned farmhouse in an advanced state of decay.

I have heard the saying "Beware the dreams of youth, for they may become the nightmares of your middle-age". What about the dreams of middle-age then, how dangerous are they, I wonder?

Eventually I suppose we will be ready to advertise for clients. Certainly our description will stand out from the crowd. For instead of declaring "Tastefully restored *fermette* with fitted kitchen and all amenities, with pool", ours will go more on these lines:

"Fermette retaining many period features" (i.e. damp walls and floors, sooty chimney-piece, low doorways whose doors change shape with the weather and won't always close).

"Experience traditional French rural life" (i.e. no phone, no washing machine, no television).

"Make friends with kindly farming folk" (i.e. smile at them even when their howling dogs wake you at night, and they rev up their tractor just when you were hoping for a lie-in).

Who will want to share our French experience? I hope to make it quite clear what facilities we do/do not offer, and to tempt clients who, like me, enjoy the simple life, even if only for a few short summer weeks. It is fabulous countryside for bird-watchers, botanists, butterfly and moth fanciers, ramblers, lovers of history and of French rural life in general. We think it is magical, but then maybe we are an odd couple! There must surely be other strange people out there – let's hope we can find them!

Time will tell. The saga continues. *Vive la France! Bon courage, mes amis!*

GLOSSARY OF FRENCH
WORDS AND PHRASES

à la votre = good health /cheers/here's to you!
avec = with
avez-vous un sac de poudre blanc? = do you have a sack of white powder?

une batteuse = a threshing machine
beau, belle = beautiful
blessé = wounded /injured
bon courage = be courageous / be brave / good luck with a
        daunting project
le bras = the arm

une camionnette = a van
ça va? = how's things / how's it going?
c'est vraiment assez = that's really enough
la chasse = the hunt (shooting)
le ciment = the cement
le compromis de vente = sale agreement

l'église = the church
encore un peu = just a little more
en panne = broken down (of a car or machine)
l'entente cordiale = friendly understanding /harmony

une fermette = small farmhouse (with farm buildings adjoining house)
une fête = a festival, celebration
une foire = a fair

fort, forte = strong

gentil, gentille = kind, nice
grand, grande = big, large
une grange = a barn
un grenier = attic, loft, hayloft

ici = here
il me donne plaisir = it pleases me, it gives me pleasure
il ne marche pas = it won't go, it doesn't work

un maçon = a mason (builder)
la maison = the house
une manifestation = a display or demonstration

un navet long = a type of long thin turnip
neuf jours de fête = nine days of celebration
le nez = the nose
non, merci = no thank you
un notaire = a notary public, French government solicitor
notre premier séjour = our first stay
nous avons un problème = we have a problem

on met du poudre blanc… = one puts some white powder…
les ordures = the domestic rubbish

pardonnez-moi = excuse me, pardon me
petit, petite = little
un permis = a permit
un pigeonnier = a pigeon house, dovecote
un placard = a cupboard

les poubelles = the rubbish bins
regarde, regardez = look (verb imperative)

un sac = a sack, a bag
la santé = health
seulement un peu = just a little
s'il vous plaît = please
une sottise = a silliness, a foolish thing
sympathique = friendly, likeable (often shortened to *sympa*)

tant pis = too bad
la terrasse = the terrace
toujours comme ça = always like that

vieux, vieille = old
voila = there you are / here it is
voulez-vous quelque chose à boire? = would you like something
        to drink?

Some of the French-based books
published by the Léonie Press:

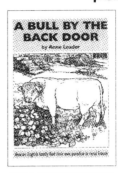

A BULL BY THE BACK DOOR
by ANNE LOADER
ISBN 1 901253 06 6 £8.99

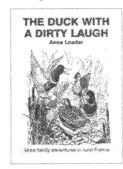

THE DUCK WITH A DIRTY
LAUGH by ANNE LOADER
ISBN 1 901253 0 90 £8.99

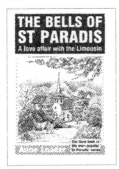

THE BELLS OF ST PARADIS
by ANNE LOADER
ISBN 1 901253 26 0 £9.99

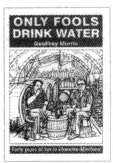

ONLY FOOLS DRINK WATER
by GEOFFREY MORRIS
ISBN 1 901253 10 4 £8.99

OU EST LE 'PING'?
by GRACE McKEE
ISBN 1 901253 11 2 £7.99

BUTTERFLIES ON MIMOSA
by ELEANOR FRANCIS
ISBN 1 901253 23 6 £8.99

LILAC AND ROSES
by PEGGY ANDERSON
ISBN 1 901253 22 8 £8.99

BANANAS IN BORDEAUX
LOUISE FRANKLIN CASTANET
ISBN 1 901253 29 5 £10.99

**COPIES FROM ANY
GOOD BOOK SHOP
OR DIRECT FROM
Léonie Press,
13 Vale Road, Hartford,
Northwich, Cheshire
CW8 1PL
Tel: 01606 75660
Fax: 01606 77609
Website:
www.leoniepress.com
E-mail:
sales@aloaderpubs.u-net.com**

184